Praise for

Full Cycle

"This is an amazing story about a remarkable family.

As a cyclist, I've fantasized plenty about embarking on a cross-country cycling adventure in a foreign land. Martha Kendall and her family actually did it!

Their journey is an inspiring reminder to pursue all your dreams — even the most implausible — and to take your family along for the ride."

Jennifer Kulier, author of
Women's Mountain Biking: A Trailside Guide

"Martha Kendall, a consummate parent, wife, teacher, and writer, takes us along on her family's 500 - mile cycling trip on Spain's *Camino de Santiago*, the medieval St. James pilgrimage trail from Roncesvalles in the Pyrenées to Santiago de Compostela in Galicia.

But most interesting of all are not the hot, dusty grain fields of Castille, or the verdant hills of Galicia, but the author's skillfully interwoven interior journey.

The title of the book is a double entendre. It's about a bike trip, but it's also about a life. If you have shared any of her experiences – and who hasn't – you'll find her story poignant and instructive … and to be remembered fondly."

Mike Booth, Travel Writer,
Granada, Spain

"Anyone who has ever been in a family will be touched by this mother's tale. Ostensibly the story of a bicycle trip across Spain, the text reveals Martha Kendall's daily demonstration of healthy parenting.

She is the emotional compass that is the hub of her family.

In her artful application of intellect, she processes her emotions while attending to the wellbeing of her children, of her husband, and of herself.

This story is a delight to read and to reflect on later. Brava!"

Barbara Ann Barnett, Ph.D., author of
365 Ways to Raise Confident Kids

"Beyond being an exquisitely told tale of an unusual journey, *Full Cycle* is the story of personal and interpersonal growth of parents and their two teenagers as they ride bicycles together across Spain.

In this engaging narrative woven with humor, intimacy, bonding and self-realization, Martha Kendall personally reveals the process of a seemingly lost art ... that of deeply sharing the journey of a nuclear family.

This is a must-read in our fragmented, multitasking, hurry-up-and-get-it-done society because, in the end, time spent equals love.

Craig W. Humphrey, Ph.D., LMHC, author of
The Heart of the Matter

Also by Martha E. Kendall

Alive in the Killing Fields, Surviving the Khmer Rouge Genocide

Benjamin Franklin

Conflict Resolution, High-interest stories that encourage critical thinking, creative writing, and dialogue

Conflict Resolution, Positive Actions for Grades K-1, 2-3 and 4-5

Elizabeth Cady Stanton, Founder of the American Women's Rights Movement

The Erie Canal

Failure Is Impossible, The History of American Women's Rights

For the Love of Chimps, The Jane Goodall Story

Herbert Hoover, America's 31st President

Inside America, Scenes of Everyday Life

John James Audubon, Artist of the Wild

Nellie Bly, Reporter for the World

Piñata Party

The Real Thing and *More of* The Real Thing, DVDs and Books that Prepare Students for College Success

Steve Wozniak, Inventor of the Apple Computer

Susan B. Anthony, Voice for Women's Voting Rights

Visit www.MarthaKendall.com
for information about these titles and
to contact the author for speaking engagements

Full Cycle

A Family's Ride Across Spain

Martha E. Kendall

Special thanks to
Alice McKown for the family biking icons,
Sandy Frye for the front cover design,
Joe Weed for the back cover design and the
maps of Spain and the Camino, and
Laura Davis for her editorial suggestions.

Printed in U.S.A.

ISBN 978-0-945783-19-0

Highland Publishing
Los Gatos, California

Full Cycle

A Family's Ride Across Spain

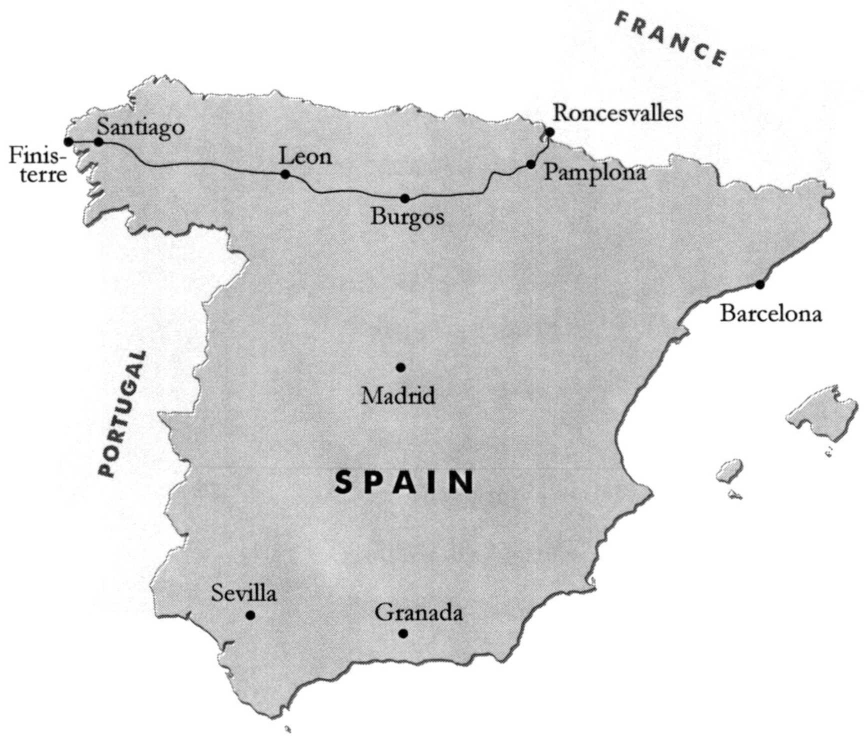

The Camino de Santiago

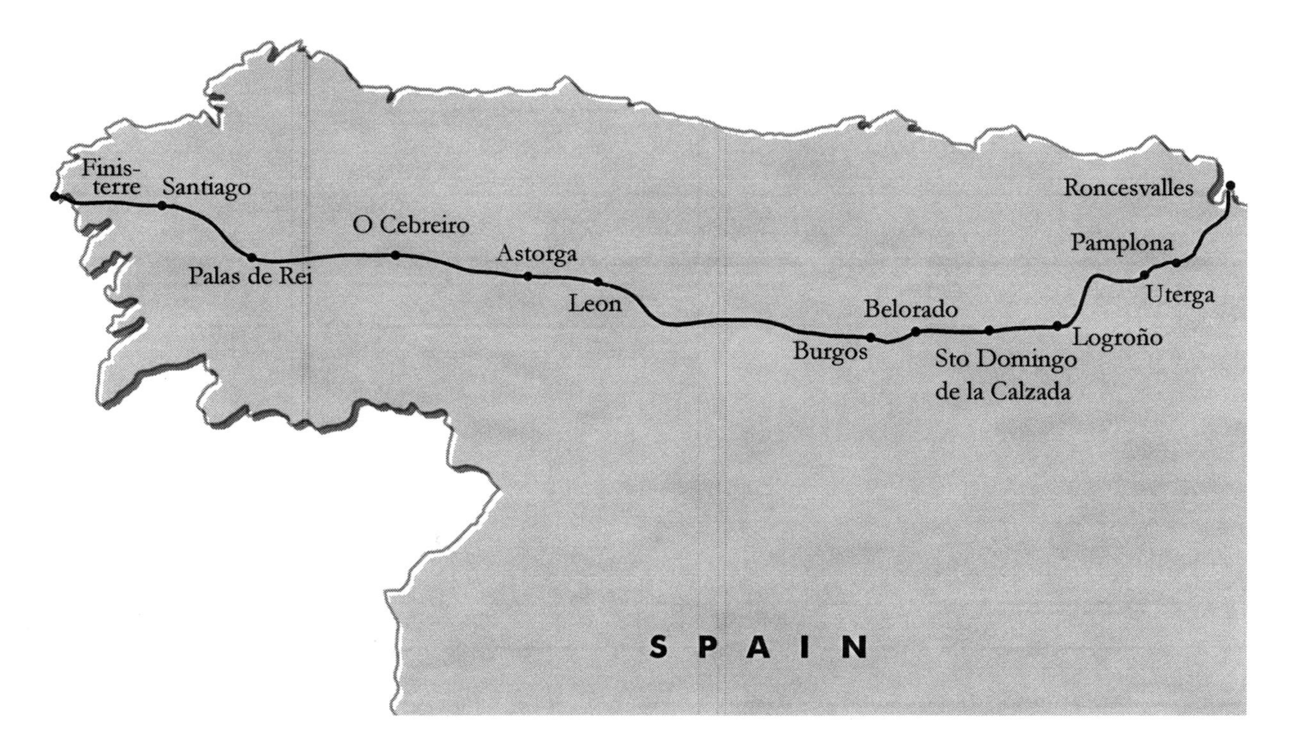
Finis-
terre
Santiago
Palas de Rei
O Cebreiro
Astorga
Leon
Burgos
Belorado
Sto Domingo
de la Calzada
Logroño
Uterga
Pamplona
Roncesvalles
SPAIN

THE WHAT?

I hold my breath and grip my handlebars.

"Tonight it begins," I murmur to Joe.

"It sure does," he says with a smile. He oozes confidence.

We're standing in the village square of Roncesvalles, a tiny Spanish town in the Pyrenées on the border with France. Lichen-covered buildings loom larger than their size warrants perhaps because their enduring existence is so unlikely in the first place. These roofed jumbles of weathered, irregular gray rocks have clung to each other for hundreds of years.

Volunteers close and lock the huge doors of the sagging building that we and a dozen other aspiring pilgrims just exited. A few of them came from France. They started their trek this morning in Saint Jean Pied de Port, just across the border. The others, like us, arrived on the late afternoon bus from points west. We will all begin our journeys at this traditional starting point. The old wooden table that we and the other pilgrims crowded around twenty minutes ago must now sit empty, awaiting the arrival of a fresh group tomorrow.

On this cool July evening, the sun is low, and dusk is overtaking the town. A few pedestrians cross the central square, but they pay little attention to us. The other pilgrims must have retired to their lodgings for the night. I don't see anyone else with bikes.

Too excited to stand still any longer, 17-year-old Jeff pedals away from us. He wheelies around the square, rearing up on his back tire like a frisky stallion in love with his testosterone. He is my self-confident charger, my I-can-do-anything Lance Armstrong. With his sandy blond hair, blue eyes, and dark eyebrows yearning to meet above his nose, he is a younger, taller version of my handsome husband.

Standing next to me, 16-year-old Katie is quiet. She is the one who least wanted to come.

Joe is the one who most wanted to.

We are about to embark on a Bicycle Ride. We plan to cross Spain from east to west, about eight hundred kilometers to Santiago, a city on the northwestern tip of the Iberian Peninsula. None of us is quite ready to start. We linger at this spot where thousands of people before us have set out on the Camino, a hiking trail created a millennium ago.

Can we do this? Can *I* do this?

Joe has been videotaping the scene, but we're losing the light. I pull out my still camera and ask a passing pedestrian to take a picture of the four of us. Katie and I hang the shells we just bought around our necks. Now we look the part, pilgrims on the Camino. The four of us line up side by side, put on our Kodak smiles, and he snaps. I thank him excessively.

Then I turn to Joe.

"Let's get going. I don't think we should ride in the dark." Joe puts his video camera away.

"To Santiago!" he says.

We cycle across the square toward the trail for the shortest leg of the trip, a mere two kilometers, downhill, to our hotel. Katie demonstrates that she still remembers from her BMX days how to bunny hop. She leaps straight up and takes her mountain bike with her.

"How did you do that?" I ask.

"It's easy, Mom. Just pull up on your handlebars, jump using your feet, and lift yourself up."

"OK. Watch this!"

Joe and Jeff look my way. I follow Katie's directions to the letter. I feel myself pull up on my handlebars, bend my knees and jump with my feet. I push my shoulders back and lift my head. But the laws of physics are cruelly insensitive. When I stopped pedaling in order to launch my mental leap off the ground, my bike, a prisoner of science, slowed down. It and I have rolled to a stop.

We all laugh.

Then we leave the square – Joe first, followed by Jeff, Katie and me. We pedal onto a leafy dirt trail shaded by a canopy of branches. It's dark and damp. The smell of decaying organic matter reminds me of soggy fall afternoons when I was a child in upstate New York. I imagine Mr. Bartolotta, my 8th grade English teacher, reciting Evangeline, "This in the forest primeval…."

As I steer around occasional roots and rocks, Joe, Jeff and Katie get farther and farther ahead of me. How do they dare to go so fast? My eyes are glued to the path. I wish I could just whistle a happy tune, but I have never mastered the whistle. I coast and brake to maintain control.

Why am I holding back? The trail is actually quite wide and generally smooth. This is not hard. The knot in my stomach loosens. I relax on my seat and hum a few bars. "Summertime, and the ridin' is easy."

In minutes, the trail deposits us on the paved, narrow main street of Burguete, another tiny mountain village. We cruise to our hotel, a picturesque tile-roofed inn with a friendly host. We're all grinning.

I can only hope it feels this good in the morning.

The next morning drips with fog. I have brought only two shirts, both of them made of high-tech, synthetic fabric that promises to wick sweat away. One is short-sleeved, white to reflect the heat and maximize my coolness factor. The other is light blue, long-sleeved, to protect me from the sun. I am wearing the blue one to protect me from the chills. When I packed, I was determined not to weigh my bike down with excess clothes. But being the daughter of an insurance man, I just had to bring a rain jacket. I zip it up and try to ignore the goose bumps on my legs. I am wearing shorts because that's all I have. Everything I read about the Camino said to beware of the heat. I wonder what other surprises are in store for us.

We huddle with our bikes on the lane outside our hotel. Katie is wearing her dark blue Dickies pants and a navy sweatshirt. I'm glad she's brought more clothes than I did. She's pulled her hair back into two short blonde braids. With her helmet on, pretty much all that shows is her lovely face, looking just the same as it did when she was a tiny girl. I wonder how much Katie and Jeff will mature in the next weeks. I wonder the same thing about myself.

How many mornings like this one await us? The answer is none, because this will be our only first one. Still unfamiliar with our saddlebags (oops, I've got to get with the cycling vocabulary; they are "panniers"), I fumble, snap, tie and re-tie my gear.

Jeff rides around, circling us on his bike. He's a hot shot cyclist. I can feel his frustration. Are we asking too much of him to tolerate our slowness, our uncoolness, our family-ness, when he would undoubtedly rather be cycling with anyone but us?

"Let's go," Jeff finally says.

Joe hops on his bike, and we all sail down the one-lane, virtually empty main street of the village. Red tiled roofs, white stucco facades, dark brown wooden doors and trim, and thriving red geraniums in every window box make the scene alpine picture perfect except for the fog. On the pavement, a spray-painted yellow arrow points to a dirt path off to the right. The Camino.

The path is narrow, so we ride single file – Jeff, then me, then Katie, then Joe. A few kilometers down the trail, we come to a wide stream crossed by a rustic wooden bridge. It's narrow, and without railings. The boards look wet and slippery. Can I get off my bike and walk across the bridge without being teased by the rest of the family?

In the lead, Jeff rides it, the boards groaning under his weight. Their vibration causes his right pannier to bounce loose from his bike. It lands in the middle of the stream.

Oh my God, if our ace rider has lost a pannier when we've barely gotten started, how are the rest of us going to fare? We haven't even been on the trail for ten minutes, and already half of Jeff's supplies are soaked. I don't believe in omens, but this is a bad one.

My maternal job description is to help everybody feel happy, loved, and safe. So what do I do now? I want to make this seem like a tiny mishap, nothing serious, no problem. Hey, this is funny! But it isn't funny. I develop a case of the shivers.

Jeff says nothing. He sits down on a boulder by the stream and takes off his shoes and socks. I walk my bike across the bridge.

"Is there anything in that pannier that'll be ruined by the water?" I ask.

He doesn't answer. He wades in without complaining about the cold or the rocks his tender feet balance on. He reaches down and grabs the soaking pannier. With his arms outstretched to keep his balance, he carefully steps back to the shore. He's hurting, but putting up a brave front. He's becoming a man. I miss my boy, even though I know I should feel nothing but pride. There's so much guilt in motherhood.

From the pannier that is still fastened on his bike, Jeff grabs a tan flannel shirt and uses it to dry himself and the dripping pannier as much as he can, which isn't much in this soggy air. Katie and then Joe walk their bikes across the bridge.

"How soaked is the stuff inside the dunked pannier?" I ask. Jeff opens the top and feels around.

"It'll be OK, Mom," he says.

I'm not sure I believe him.

"Good for you, honey," I say, wrapping my arms around my mid-section. Then, groping for anything positive, "You've always been adaptable." He glances at me and says "Huh?" in his articulate adolescent argot. He sits on the boulder again and starts putting his socks and shoes back on.

"I remember the time when you were about three and you stripped off all your clothes *except* for your shoes and socks," I say.

"C'mon, Mom," he says, "I don't want to hear a story about me being naked."

"You said, 'I'm going to sunbathe.' I told you it was pretty cloudy for sunbathing. You answered, 'OK, I'll cloud bathe.' You strode onto the deck, sprawled out on the lounge chair and lay there, face and everything else up, for almost a full twenty seconds. I think you were bored after ten, but you wanted to make a point."

"I'm bored now. Let's go ridin'," Jeff says.

We do.

Jeff has always loved to "go ridin'." While I watch his 17-year-old physique as he pedals his green Bontrager mountain bike, I can still see him as a four-year-old riding a neighbor's faded yellow hand-me-down tricycle. For Jeff, it was love at first bike. He lived on it. I think his Y chromosome included the ability to careen around corners, leaning his little torso parallel with the pavement. His feet twirled the trike's pedals while his mouth exuded the sound of a Harley.

When Jeff was six, a family friend gave him a two-wheeler, a bright red girl's Schwinn she found at a garage sale for ten dollars. Jeff needed training wheels for about seven and a half minutes. Then he was free, and he has been ever since.

We ride through a couple of little towns, really just clusters of a few stone and stucco buildings. One or two locals glance at us, and flocks of sparrows chirp a greeting. Often the trail descends. After all, we're starting in the Pyrenées and heading toward the Plains of Spain, so our first days ought to be spent generally coasting downhill. But I'm seeing a significant "up" right ahead. I recall reading that Spain is the second most mountainous country in Europe. At least we won't have to scale the Alps.

The path narrows and climbs a rocky hill so steep even Jeff gets off and pushes his bike. Our elbows rub against the scrub brush lining the trail. Whenever I stop to rest, I hold the brake levers so my bike doesn't backslide. This trail would suit a 15-year-old Boy Scout working on a merit badge. I am a 55-year-old Baby Boomer working off my adrenaline. Ahead of us, a couple of walking pilgrims trudge up the hill, but they have only themselves to move forward. My bike seems like a beast of burden – my burden.

At the top, we get back on, and pedal and pedal and pedal. Minutes turn into hours as we negotiate the changing terrain. I have never ridden a bike this long before. My thigh muscles are mushifying. And I thought we had prepared for the trip! We did train, but not for this. My hands tingle, threatening to fall asleep from the lack of blood, I suppose a result of the angle my wrists are bent. I huff up the hills. When I'm not braking on the descents, I shake out my hands.

Sometimes the path follows the margin of a sloping field. Then it cuts through a village and becomes bike- and bone-rattling cobblestones. After we pass a dozen or so buildings, the lane morphs into a tractor trail through the countryside. I am focused on staying upright and keeping my wheels spinning on all these bumpy, rutted surfaces. We haven't seen any other cyclists. Maybe they know another route? Or maybe there aren't other cyclists?

Now the path has merged with a narrow paved road, old and seemingly empty. It weaves along a mountainside, damp and lush with evergreens. Except for the occasional pilgrim hiker carrying a backpack, where are all the people?

We cross a weathered stone bridge leading into a village and spot our first grocery store, by American standards a tiny corner market.

Joe says, "Let's stop to get lunch supplies."

"Great idea," says Jeff, who is always hungry.

For the last five or eight or ten miles – a really long time is all I am sure of – I have been ready to take a break for any reason. Hallelujah, we have arrived somewhere.

"Sure, let's take a look," I say in my best Ms. Casual, positive role model voice.

We lean our bikes against the building and troop inside the store. I have no idea what time it is, but Jeff and Katie say as they high five, "It's sandwich time."

Joe takes on a talkative persona in his excellent Spanish. He smiles, relishing the interaction with a polite shopkeeper who does not stare at our funny-looking American clothes and cycling shoes. After much more discussion than is needed, and with a look of joy that seems a bit over the top for the practical exchange that has just occurred, Joe pays for a baguette, cheese, salami, orange juice, yogurt, fruit and chocolates.

With our purchases in hand, we go outside to picnic by the river we just crossed. On the far shore, a white wagtail scurries about, living up to its name by bobbing its tail nonstop. I carefully settle on a rock that's angled enough not to be holding any puddles, and I cover my legs with my rain jacket.

We inhale the food and marvel that we just rode over a Roman bridge.

"Can anybody ballpark when this bridge was built, give or take five hundred years?" I ask.

"When the Romans wanted to get to the other side," says Katie.

"Romans occupied parts of Spain for about seven hundred years, starting in 200 BC," says Joe, who studied Spanish history as a student at the University of Granada.

I jump on this opportunity to teach about literature. "Then this bridge was here when the Battle of Roncesvalles was fought in the late 8th Century. The story of the battle is told in France's oldest manuscript, *La Chanson de Roland*, the 'Song of Roland.'"

"Are you going to sing it, Mom?" asks Katie.

"*Quand il me prend dans ses bras, il me parle tout bas, La Chanson de Roland.*"

"Edith Piaf never sang it like that," says Joe with a wink.

"What?" says Jeff between bites.

"That's a famous French song, '*La Vie en Rose.*' I changed the words a little. 'The Song of Roland' is a poem based on a legend about Charlemagne's retreat back to France after he failed to defeat the Muslims in Spain."

"This Christian-Muslim thing wasn't invented on 9/11," says Jeff.

"It's been around for more than a thousand years, and Santiago – "

Katie interrupts. "It's called 'The Song of Roland,' but it's about Charlemagne?"

"It's mostly about Charlemagne's nephew, Roland. He led the rear guard of Charlemagne's army, which got ambushed. Everybody under Roland's command, including Roland, was killed in Roncesvalles," I say.

"Let's ride in the front guard," Katie says.

Jeff stands, wiping his hands on his shorts. "Great idea. Let's go ridin'."

Once we're cycling again, I feel like we are cruising right along. How can this be, when I should be more than totally beyond exhausted? Our practice rides at home never lasted more than about an hour and a half, maybe two at the most. This morning's effort was Herculean, but now I've got a second wind. It seems doubtful that we have descended so much that the lower elevation makes it easier to breathe. Perhaps it is because at lunch I indulged in comfort food. I like salami, no matter that I can hear a well-informed NPR commentator say, "It is filled with fat. The bad kind!" I've just eaten lots of it and am feeling good.

The air is still chilly and damp, but the food in my belly and the exertion from riding keep me warm. There's no sun, but I bask in appreciation that it's not raining. None of these little villages has had anything like a *pension* or hotel, so onward we must roll, no matter the weather.

A small flock of European goldfinches skitters past, the males' red faces much brighter than the yellow and black American goldfinches I'm used to seeing. On a dirt tractor trail, we pass a beautiful misty green pasture where a half dozen chestnut draft horses interrupt their grazing to gaze at us. Healthy and calm and doing what horses are supposed to do, they embody the idyllic bliss I imagined I would find in the Pyrenées. The scene looks just like the painting I admired in the hotel dining room this morning – a long time ago. Now we are experiencing the Camino face to face and foot to pedal, not reading about it or looking at pictures of it.

One night a few months back, a friend of Joe's parents came for dinner. He had cycled the Camino route, riding on roads that parallel the trail. His photos showed lovely villages, spectacular panoramas of mountains and farmland, and cathedrals whose architecture reflected changing fashions over the past thousand years. He said the people he met were seeking a physical or spiritual journey, or in his case, a good time and good exercise. Joe is determined that we ride mountain bikes on the Camino trail itself, not on the roads nearby.

At this moment, I think roads sound very appealing. The trail has just changed to single track, which Jeff loves. He and Katie lead the way. I am trying not to freak out about this single track, a groove that measures ten inches wide. No, I exaggerate. It's four inches wide. I tune in my personal pep talk voice. "You have a good sense of balance. Just stay in the groove, and you won't have a problem."

I brake to maneuver around a rock, and my tire hits the edge of the track. My bike and I keel over. Daredevil that I am not, I've been going about two miles per hour, and my bike and I land on tall, dense, dew-covered grass. I lie there thankful that I am not hurt. Prince Charming arrives on the scene. Without any chiding (I do love this man), Joe leans down and pulls my white Trek and me, intimately wrapped up in each other, back into a vertical position on the trail.

"Let's not mention to Katie or Jeff that I've already fallen," I say. Joe nods and leans across his bike to give me a kiss.

"When I fell off a horse, I always got back on," I say. Using his gloved hands, Joe helps me brush damp grass off my shorts and jacket.

We resume pedaling to catch up to the kids, but I can't repress the what-ifs. I could have broken my leg and ruined the trip on our first day, destroying Joe's dream and our family's chance to tackle our greatest physical and emotional adventure.

To my relief, the single track ends. It has led us to another almost empty paved road that descends gently through a narrow valley. This is my kind of cycling. I shake the tingles out of my right hand, and then the left. I remember the mantra of my horseback riding coach when I was a teenager, "Take a deep seat and let your mind wander." I dare to let my eyes wander as I coast on the smooth pavement. The landscape looks very similar to the hillsides by our northern California home. I savor the smells-just-right aroma of pine trees and pristine air. Joe is in the rear, and I brake to wait for him. Keeping my what-if worries to myself, I return his grin.

"I guess it's all easy ridin' from here," I say.

He points the video camera cradled in his right arm toward me. While he records the present, I flash to the past that brought us to this moment.

Joe took up bicycling six years ago because of a troublesome knee that made our daily jogs painful for him. When Jeff moved up to a better mountain bike, Joe started riding the one he's on now, Jeff's hand-me-down, a dark green, off-brand Motiv.

I glance at Jeff in the lead, his posture relaxed. He's used to being in front, or close to it, in BMX, downhill, cross-country, dual slalom, and cyclo-cross races. All I wanted was for him to have fun on his bike and not get hurt. He wanted to win a spot on the podium, which he often did. William Blake said that you don't know how much is enough until you've had too much, but Jeff is nowhere near his cycling "too much" point.

The descent ends, yet I still pedal easily. Pavement is my new best friend.

I ask Joe, who's still riding fairly close to me, "Did you think it would be like this?"

"It's even better!"

"How does this compare to Rattlesnake Gulch?"

"Even better!"

I picture Joe and Jeff riding that steep, rugged trail on a Saturday last winter. The Gulch is a notoriously rough downhill run a couple of miles from our house, and Joe was trying it for the first time. I imagine Jeff in the lead, going slow enough that Joe could keep up, but fast enough to show off his technical skills. When they got home, Joe looked wiped out, and Jeff was rarin' for more. Their jackets, legs and faces were splattered with dirt. They were both beaming, having attained a manly Nirvana together.

That night, after the kids were in their rooms, Joe and I met in the kitchen to unwind from the day and enjoy a glass of wine. Because Joe spends much of his time seated at his recording console, and I spend much of my time seated as I grade essays, we like to stand up when we take breaks. On this particular evening, we leaned against the kitchen counter.

Joe broached the subject. "Jeff said today that he'd be interested in cycling the Camino de Santiago next summer."

"The what?"

"The Camino in Spain. It's a pilgrimage trail that crosses the country from east to west," he said. "I've always wanted to do it."

"A pilgrimage?" I asked.

"It's a car-free route, a hiking trail, created a thousand years ago. It goes from France to the shrine for Santiago, Spain's patron saint." Joe ran downstairs to his studio and returned carrying a small book. He opened it and showed me, in his handwriting, "*Un día, lo haré.*" "One day, I will do it." He had signed his name, Joe Weed, and dated it "July 1970," the summer after his junior year abroad at the University of Granada.

He said, "I photocopied the book and had the pages bound. It's the first published travel guide to the Camino, written in the 12th Century. I've been thinking about this a lot. Jeff and I can cycle it. Would you like to rent a car in Madrid, cruise the roadways near the Camino with Katie, and meet us at each overnight stop?" I held up my glass for a refill. He poured me more Chardonnay and topped up his glass with Sauvignon Blanc.

"This is a big idea. I need to sidle up to it." I took another sip. "It sure would give Katie and me a lot of time together. Maybe she's just being a typical 15-year-old, but she doesn't talk to me as much as she used to. The two of us in a car would be great." I imagined us solving the problems of the world as we drove, enjoying extended lunches at picturesque cafés, browsing in cute shops, and in the evenings, laughing as Joe and Jeff recounted their tales from the trail. But wait. I wanted to have tales, too, beyond describing the day's food intake, a souvenir we didn't buy, or how lost we got trying to read the map. Surely Katie and I could be more than a sag wagon ladies' auxiliary.

I took a gulp of my Chardonnay, working up the courage to ask, "Do you think it would be possible for all of us to ride together, or would it be way too hard for Katie and me?"

"That would be wonderful!" said Joe. He looked like he'd opened a birthday present he hadn't dared to hope for. "I'm sure we can find lots of information about it."

"We can research it tomorrow, but for tonight, let's sleep on it," I said. We clinked our glasses and finished the wine.

Before falling asleep in our undulating waterbed, I mulled the idea over. I loved the prospect of returning to

Spain, a country Joe and I had twice visited pre-kids. I was also lured by the chance to speak Spanish. The last time we'd traveled to a Spanish-speaking country was to attend the wedding of a nephew in the family I had lived with when I was a high school summer exchange student in Mexico. Jeff, then 15, had been remarkably outgoing using his high school Spanish with the family's teenage cousins. Katie had seemed less comfortable, but she'd had a good time.

Could a long, demanding cycling journey be fun, or even feasible, for all of us? I would hate to have Katie hate it, and I would hate to be such a klutz I'd spoil everybody else's fun. Maybe I should retract my ego, bow out, and support Joe and Jeff in tackling a great challenge together. Or maybe I should have the ovaries to make this a grand experience for the whole family. So far, we had never had a family trip that had gone wrong. How could this one be any different? After all, I married Mr. Right.

"Look," says Mr. Right, jolting me back to the present. He points toward the distance. Ahead of us, the sun is breaking through the fog. The turrets, roofs, and steeples of Pamplona sparkle below. We have cycled down and up and down more than fifty miles.

"Unbelievably beautiful" I shout.

At a wide spot in the lane, we pedal four abreast. I call out, "Hurray for Team Kendall-Weed!" Jeff wheelies, Katie lifts her left hand to make a quick thumbs-up before grabbing back onto her handlebars, and Joe videotapes the valley in front of us. No matter how many miles remain until we settle into a hotel in Pamplona, we will pedal them bathed in sunshine and affirmation.

SAINT JAMES

"I'd really like to have a Camelbak like Jeff's," says Katie while we're eating breakfast.

"You're kind of young for a widow's hump," I say. She doesn't bother to roll her eyes, because she knows I know what she means – a small rucksack designed to hold water that a tube carries on demand to the mouth of the cyclist. The key here is not its function, but the fact that Jeff has one.

"Sure, honey. Let's see if we can find one." I repress the urge to comment that it would have been a lot easier if she'd made this request back in California.

"Why don't you get one, too?" she suggests. I feel like a heel for being so quick to criticize her.

"I'm doing fine with my water bottle," I say.

Joe does not contest my easy acquiescence to her request. He asks the hotel manager if there's a bike shop nearby. Fortunately, there is. We can indulge Katie and then get our second day of cycling under way. We follow the manager's directions to the shop, which turns out to be only about half a mile from our hotel. The shop owner recognizes the term Camelbak. I wonder if he has any idea what Camelbak means in English, or if he's just memorized the name. He explains that he has none in stock, but he suggests we try a larger sporting goods store at a new shopping center on the outskirts of the city.

That there's a strong possibility of finding what Katie wants is the good news. The bad news is that to get to the store requires riding about ten kilometers, on crowded city streets, in the wrong direction away from the Camino. Joe and I exchange glances. Is this digression really necessary?

"Let's look at the map," I say to Joe and huddle close to him. As I expected, Katie tunes out as soon as she hears the word "map," and her attention is taken by a bright orange cycling shirt that she points out to Jeff. While the kids are distracted, Joe and I caucus.

"Remember Robert Pirsig," I whisper. I don't need to say, it's the journey, not the destination.

"Of course," he answers. I should have known that words were not necessary. We both know that Katie has no particular affinity for long distance biking, and we want to help make this trip a positive experience for her.

On the sidewalk in front of the bike shop, Joe says, "Listen up, everybody. We're going to be riding in traffic. We need to be visible." He reaches into his pannier and pulls out four clip-on red lights. "Push the button until the light flashes, and then clamp it onto the back of your pannier."

We do as he says, and head out. Protectively, he rides last. We dodge cars on busy streets. This feels dangerous. The road widens to a 6-lane highway, and traffic zooms past us. I am skeptical bikes are allowed. If they are, they shouldn't be. We pedal for about 45 minutes until we find the place. Surrounded by expansive parking lots, the store is one of many under the roof of a new, ugly, all-too-familiar conglomeration of big box outlets. Is Spain getting malled American-style?

"Time is slipping away," Joe says. "How about if some of us buy the Camelbak, and you buy lunch?"

"Good plan," I say. Joe and I are totally connecting, underplaying the fact that it's already early afternoon, and we have not only failed to continue our westward journey, we have also cycled away from the trail.

"I need to go into the store to see the Camelbaks," says Katie. Jeff has already chained his bike to a post, taken off his helmet, and is walking toward the mall entrance.

While Joe and the kids seek the Camelbak, I keep an eye on the bikes and buy sandwiches and juice drinks from a sidewalk vendor. I wait for an eternity, or at least fifteen minutes, until Joe, Jeff and Katie emerge carrying the dromedarian holy grail in a plastic bag.

We picnic on a peninsula of grass. No family meal is complete without pleasant conversation, particularly when we're dining in a parking lot.

"Who remembers why Santiago is Spain's patron saint?" I ask.

"Because his name starts with 's'," Jeff says.

"Good a reason as any." I'm sure Joe knows the whole story, but he's letting me enjoy my teacher role.

"The legend is that Saint James a.k.a. San Diego a.k.a. Santiago probably never even came here, at least when he was technically alive."

"Life is a technicality," says Katie.

I take another bite of my sandwich.

"After Saint James died, his remains were sent in a stone boat that traveled, without a sail or oars, to a beach on Spain's northwestern coast. A bridegroom, who just happened to be passing by, was amazed by the sight of this strange boat and did the only thing he could do – he rode his horse into the sea. They would have drowned except that Santiago miraculously caused them to emerge safe and sound, fully covered in shells. So that's why pilgrims wear shells today."

Joe adds, "A lot of the early pilgrims were French, and they brought their shells home with them. They created 'coquilles Saint-Jacques,' scallops of Saint James, a dish that they served on the shell."

"Let's try making that when we get back," says Katie, who loves to cook almost as much as she loves to eat.

"Speaking of food – " Jeff says. He gets up and strolls to his bike. He reaches in his pannier and pulls out four Clif bars.

"Jeff, you are your generous, well prepared father's son," I say. He hands a high energy snack bar to each of us.

After thirty years of giving college lectures, I am not about to let this one go unfinished. This unexpected dessert provides the time I need.

"The body of Saint James was supposedly buried at Santiago de Compostela a century after he died in Jerusalem. Compostela, 'Field of Stars,' may have gotten its name because in the ninth century, eight hundred years after Santiago was buried, a religious hermit named Pelayo said he saw a glowing star over a field that he said must be Santiago's unmarked grave. Pelayo talked to the Bishop, who ordered construction of the cathedral at that spot."

"Do you think we should keep an eye out for a glowing star?" asks the Mistress of Sarcasm.

"I think *you* are a glowing star," answers the Mother of Sentimentality.

"Let's go ridin'," says Jeff.

I finger the Santiago shell I'm wearing as a necklace. "*Shell* we hit the trail? Yuk Yuk Yuk." I'm imitating my grandmother's best friend Myrtle. She laughed in distinctly articulated, deep rrr's and uh's that sounded more like a coughing spasm than a spontaneous giggle. Because many of my puns are so bad nobody else laughs at all, I take responsibility for doing so, Myrtle style. Or, instead of bothering to imitate her, I just say, "Myrtle laugh."

It is late afternoon by the time we have cycled back through the traffic-jammed streets of Pamplona to resume our ride on the Camino. It is much more to my liking. The dirt trail immediately climbs away from the city, bordering a field packed with west-facing yellow sunflowers. They smile at us, encouraging our progress. I flash to the memory of the matching mother/daughter dresses Katie and I chose from the Penney's catalog when she was about seven. They were navy and white checked with a sunflower at the neckline. We wore them to family parties, when she played in a summer recital, and sometimes at home just for fun. Here we are now, not wearing sunflowers but pedaling past them on the other side of the world.

Yesterday we saw dozens of hikers on the trail, but this afternoon we are totally alone. I bet the walkers left the city early in the morning, so they are already well along on the day's hike. When we pause for Katie and me to take off our jackets, I ask Joe, "Do you think we should be concerned about our getting to a town with a place to stay before it gets dark?" I am pretending that the kids can't catch my subtext, Are we going to get lost in these mountains tonight?

Joe carries the guidebook in his pannier and keeps a map in a plastic pouch velcroed on top of his handlebar bag.

"The map shows it's only about twenty kilometers from here to Uterga, and the guidebook says there are *pensiones* there."

"That's about thirteen or fourteen miles?"

"We can do it, easy," he says. "I bet once we get to the top of this ridge that we'll be able to see Uterga in the distance."

"How about a kiss, Mr. Optimist?"

"Eeew," says Katie. "Look away, Jeff. The parents are getting physical."

We all get physical as we work our way up the climb. There is no sweeping vista once we huff our way to the top of this ridge. Instead, we see more ridges. We ascend one after another and then spy a row of long-armed silver windmills atop the highest one. These are not the Dutch-style windmills of Don Quijote's fantasies. I imagine having to ride under them at just the right time so as not to be sliced by their rotating knife-like arms. We near these techno turbines, and their whirring grows louder, eerie testament to their size and power. They have been erected in the right place. The wind is strong and steady, and we put our outer layers back on.

The trail veers off to the right, dodging the steel monsters. We come across a rust-colored two-dimensional metal sculpture that depicts larger-than-life pilgrims heading westward, leaning into the wind with their garments billowing behind them. We pose with the sculptured pilgrims, our jackets billowing, too. From here, the trail drops off, becoming a wild jumble of loose rocks, cobbles and stones that blanket the steep hillside.

As I start down, I concentrate on the most basic of biking skills – keeping my balance. Two things definitely need improvement. Please help me, Dr. Seuss. Thing One is my cycling competence, and Thing Two is my cycling confidence. I agree completely with Lance Armstrong that "It's not about the bike." It is about me, and I'm a loser. I am taking forever to maneuver my way down this skiddy, always moving surface. Balancing on marbles would be easier. They'd be all the same size. There's no way to get traction on these unstable rocks and pebbles. I am way too focused on managing my handlebars to observe how Jeff and Joe, ahead of me, are handling it. I brake, skid, barely balance, and try to think of alternative ways to deal with this challenge. Like maybe getting off my bike and giving it a downhill shove. I could stumble my way down, or glissade as if this were a snow slope, and meet my bike at the bottom.

I yell to Katie behind me, "How are you doing?" It will be a miracle in this wind if she can even hear me.

She yells back, saying either, "This sucks!" or "This rocks!" I agree. These rocks suck.

I don't risk my almost-balance to turn around to look at her. I keep on going, going, going, every few feet equal to light years in breathless anxiety. I can not allow myself to fall, to get hurt, to wreck the trip for everybody on our second day out.

Finally, the steepness decreases. I dare to look up and see Joe and Jeff waiting at the bottom of the hill. Katie arrives moments after I do. I breathe deeply.

Jeff looks bored. Katie calmly sips from her Camel-bak.

"That was a bit of a challenge, don't you think?" I ask Joe. My personal pride monitor prevents me from saying, "Oh My God, this is a miracle we all survived that descent!"

"You did fine," Joe says.

Hmm. "Fine." Nobody else appears to feel like we've just succeeded at something that was terrifying. Katie looks as bored as Jeff. I'm the only one who has had an internal crisis. I thought my role as Mom would be to help everybody keep a positive attitude, and I'm the one who seems to have an attitude problem.

My mature self, trying to feel sassy, scolds me: Drama Queen, just calm down. It wasn't that big of a deal. Relax.

My sissy self shudders: Relax? Who are you trying to kid? It was only thanks to complete luck that I have not had a serious crash so far.

Sassy: Are you a 55-year-old toddler, the poster child for pusillanimity? Grow up.

Sissy: I'll try. Really.

We start pedaling again. I am more than relieved that the Camino has morphed from an unridable erosion chute into none other than a virtually empty paved road. What bliss! How safe and civilized! *Viva españa!* I suspect that all pilgrims over the centuries have appreciated traveling where the Camino is safe and civilized.

I picture us in the context of hundreds of years' worth of pilgrims. If we succeed on this ride, we will fulfill one of Joe's lifelong dreams. How many other pilgrims have made this trip to fulfill a dream? I like thinking about the people before us, a thousand years' worth of people, traveling these same ancient roads, footpaths and bridges. I like the continuity of travelers experiencing a physical and emotional journey, heading west, creating their own destinies. The history of Santiago does not define our odyssey. We do.

Santiago's history drips with blood. When his shrine was built in 900, Muslims outnumbered Christians in northern Spain. Encouraging pilgrims to travel into the region boosted the church's influence. Then a Spanish King, Ramiro, had a dream in which Santiago went one step farther. Besides being a pilgrim to his own shrine, he became a *Matamoros*, the Killer of Moors. He rode a white horse into battles where he wielded a shining sword. Our shells have red dagger-like crosses painted on them.

I am not a pilgrim who honors this "saint." I'm a traveler trying my best to help my family succeed on this ride with joy and gusto. This trip is tightening our bonds. The glue is love.

Although a hit movie claimed that "Love means never having to say you're sorry," sometimes it means having to say "no." During the rainy winter when 10-year-old Jeff couldn't ride his bike outside very much, he heard his friends talk about karate, practiced indoors. He wanted to give it a try, so we signed him up. He learned the moves, memorized the patterns, yelled "Ay-yah," did push-ups, passed the tests, and moved up from white belt to yellow to green to purple to orange to brown to red/black. In sixth grade he earned his black belt. Then, he wanted to try something new: a motorcycle.

No.

We settled on a compromise. Motorcyclists in Moto-Cross races roar around tracks built up with jumps that send the riders and their motorcycles flying through the air. Bicycle Moto-Cross, called BMX, is a scaled down, pedal-powered version of the sport. We got a BMX bike for Jeff. It had 20" wheels, and only one gear. Like the other BMXers, Jeff pedaled wildly around a short, jump-filled dirt oval. He raced at the BMX track in Santa Clara and accumulated dozens of trophies. We took him to a handful of national competitions, too. He won a 3' tall trophy when he came in first in his age group, 11-year-olds, in the intermediate category at the Santa Barbara Nationals.

Our champ loved winning races, but he came to love jumping even more, just for the joy of it. At a Cupertino park, he and his bike flew off the ground from dirt take-off ramps he and his friends had dug and shoveled between the oaks. We drove him to indoor skate parks that allowed bikes and he swooped and sailed at indoor ramp clubs.

As a teenager, Jeff and his buddies would pedal hard up their launch ramps and then fly many feet in the air before thumping back down on solid ground. I cringed at their death defying in-air stunts: no handers, no footers, kick outs, X-ups and Superman seat grabs. My vocabulary, if not my nerve, was growing by leaps and bounds.

I couldn't pretend everything was a perfect picture of athletic guys enjoying a wholesome sport. I remember the anxiety I felt when I brought this up with Joe.

"I think we should talk to Jeff about the BMX crowd," I said, "and we probably should have ages ago."

"What's wrong with them?" asked Joe.

"These kids are nice to me, but they are disaffected with school. They are outsiders. They swear in every sentence, and sometimes I catch a whiff of dope. I can't believe I'm dropping Jeff off to hang out with them," I said with obvious guilt.

"Do you think Jeff is smoking?"

"Not at all. You know how he doesn't even drink soda or eat desserts. He says, 'Duh, that stuff is bad for you.' So I don't think he'd smoke dope."

"Jeff better deserve our trust," said Joe.

"If we question him about being involved with drugs, and he isn't, he'll think we don't have faith in him. Nobody rises to low expectations."

Joe pondered this, but I interrupted his thoughts.

"Oedipus lives. Jeff will be defensive if you talk to him."

"Yes, you do it," said Joe.

The next evening, I volunteered to do the dishes so Joe could go back down to his studio, Katie could do homework up in her room, and Jeff could finish his homework at the dining room table. As I poured the soap into the dishwasher, I said as conversationally as I could, "Honey, have you ever noticed that in some ways you seem a little different from the other BMX guys?" He burst out laughing, seeing right through my exquisitely crafted question.

"Of course, Mom!" he said. "I'm not like them and I never will be. We just like to ride bikes together."

By the time I get a handle on a stage he's going through, he is on to the next one. Jeff has never been a follower, and I should have realized he wouldn't follow the other BMXers. He has always done his own thing, with other kids following him. In fact, when Katie was very little, she tried to do whatever her big brother did. At one and a half, she would stand in front of the toilet pretending to pee.

As for cycling, Katie tried BMX for a few months when Jeff was racing a lot, and she won a first place trophy. But Katie preferred soccer to cycling. She was a star goalie until her knee gave way due to more injuries than I want to remember. Spinning wheels, the doctors assured us, would be the ideal exercise for her knee this summer.

Ah, sweet Katie. What a good-hearted girl she is to be here at all. When Joe first talked about the Camino, she said nothing. Her idea of a day well spent was sleeping 'til noon, then eating mint chocolate chip ice cream while rereading a John Grisham mystery for the third time. Spending days slogging on a many-hundred-mile bike trip was not what I would predict would be her first choice "vacation" activity. I recall one afternoon when Joe and I came into the house sweaty and still panting after biking up our steep driveway. Katie commented, "Interesting what you choose to do for fun." I didn't want to tell her she *had* to do this with us. I wanted her to *want* to do it. I suggested to Joe that we plan an easy ride that would end with dinner at the kids' favorite restaurant. If that outing were fun for all of us, "everybody" might get excited – or at least feel OK – about the idea of spending weeks riding together.

We set the plan in action. The four of us headed out from home on a crisp Saturday early in the spring. The winding old road lined by redwoods was virtually car-free. It would be a fifteen-mile jaunt, almost all downhill from our ridge top house to the village of Corralitos where we had parked our van, not far from Manuel's Mexican restaurant on the beach.

The noisiest member of the family, I hummed my favorite Patsy Cline tune, "Walkin' After Midnight." I inhaled the moist forest air, laughed at the bobbing styrofoam Jack in the Box head that Jeff had tied to the top of his helmet, and slalomed to capture the feeling of cutting curves on Sierra ski slopes. It was the kind of glorious, great-to-be-alive afternoon when flightless kiwis take wing and mute swans discover their inner soprano. With my heart overflowing, I turned and grinned at the handsomest man in the world. His red lumberjack shirt flapped in the breeze. No fancy schmancy spandex for him.

Katie was cycling slowly, so I braked to wait for her, bursting with love and exuberance. Was she also exhilarated by this moment, this place, this family? Did she have more than an inkling about how good her life, our lives, were?

"How are you doing, honey?" I asked enthusiastically as we coasted near each other.

"Fine," she answered, the picture of politeness. Her eyes stayed focused on the road.

After we made it to Corralitos and loaded our bikes into the van, I knew there would be no better time to talk about the Camino. I was determined to create a positive context for the conversation. One of my cello teachers showed me that no note is hard. It's getting *to* it that can be tricky. So, I would lead up to the question so that when we got to it, a "yes" answer would come easily.

As soon as Joe turned on the ignition, I started reminiscing about our month cruising the Erie Canal across upstate New York when the kids were in third and fourth grade. We leased the Van Rensselaer, a long, narrow steel-hulled boat. Our floating home served as our means of transportation, if you can call five miles per hour "going" anywhere. Joe handled the tiller as smoothly as if it had been a bow he was using to fiddle the Sailor's Hornpipe. After observing Joe call lockkeepers on our marine band radio to ask for passage, Jeff begged to do the same. In his nine-year-old voice, he'd hold the radio button and say, "Calling Lock Nine, Lock Nine, this is the Van Rensselaer westbound. Requesting passage, Sir."

"We're ready for you, Captain," the lockmaster would answer. "The gates are open."

"Thank you, Sir," Jeff answered, his voice a step lower as he coolly replaced the radio on its hook. After Joe maneuvered us into a lock, I would walk to the bow to grab the guide rope dangling down the lock wall. Jeff would join me to supervise. As for Katie, she usually kept her nose in a book. Between the locks and low bridges she sometimes surprised us with popcorn snacks or ants on a log, a celery stick filled with peanut butter and topped with raisins. When we docked in towns along the way, Katie reminded us how important it was to sample the local ice cream, prompting sweet temptation and deliverance. We cruised in the past lane, with no TV, telephone or internet. We truly had each other for company.

After we were seated at Manuel's and were waiting for our salads, I launched into anecdotes about our two-week odyssey on Alaska's Inside Passage. A hammer dulcimer player on a cruise ship had hired Joe to contribute fiddle, and I played guitar and sang harmony with her. We had a common repertoire of traditional American music, from Turkey in the Straw to Arkansas Traveler. Of course we brought Jeff and Katie along on the cruise. They charmed the other passengers by doing magic tricks for free, and they charged a dime if people wanted to find out the "trick to the tricks." Most of them did. With her fees and tips, Katie bought me a souvenir coffee mug. She also performed with us, fiddling Golden Slippers and wearing a pair, too. Jeff got his moment of glory during the talent show when he gave a karate demonstration and broke boards Joe held up for him.

When my enchilladas arrived, I changed forks and subjects. "I wonder what Cap'n Bob's up to these days?" I asked. He was the gravelly voiced pilot who took us up the Mississippi in his vintage wooden trawler. He wanted company as he traveled from St. Louis to his homeport in Minneapolis. For three weeks, we cruised the Mother of Waters with him, spending the nights in marinas Katie and I chose. Joe and I performed a few small concerts in river towns, and Jeff made instant friends with local riders who spotted his BMX bike on the boat's deck even before we docked. Katie was inspired to write "The Adventures of Becky Thatcher" after we left Hannibal.

"Flan, anyone?" the waitress asked.

"Sure," I said, opting for calories to buy time to talk about the fun we'd had on other trips. Katie asked for Mexican chocolate ice cream, Joe ordered coffee, and Jeff as usual turned down any sweets.

The waitress brought the check before I had a chance to recall much about our mule ride in Zion National Park, our house boating adventure way down upon the Suwannee River, or our canoeing with alligators in a Louisiana Bayou.

I suspected Katie saw through my efforts to arouse enthusiasm for another family trip. As Joe paid the bill, I popped the question.

"Katie, do you think you could enjoy a family cycling trip across Spain?"

"Sure," she said. I felt that in her heart she really wasn't interested, but her congenial nature prompted her to say what she knew we wanted to hear. I could only hope her agreement would not be something she would later regret.

I am pulled from that memory into the present. We have pedaled up a hill. At the top of the rise, I see no sign indicating that this is Uterga, where a *pension* is supposed to be. There are a few buildings, and a lovely old church stands on our right. Its beige stonework, trimmed green lawn and bright orange bird of paradise flowers create a stunning scene with a panorama of the tilled valley behind it.

"I bet that pilgrims have admired this spot for hundreds of years. Doesn't it feel good to be part of a tradition that goes back so far?"

"Yup," says Jeff agreeably.

A seesaw stands at the edge of the church's well-kept

grounds, so my teenagers try it out.

After a few ups and downs, Katie says, "I'm starving. I'm exhausted."

She gets off the seesaw and lies down on her back, sprawled under a shade tree. She closes her eyes.

"I hope Uterga is close," I say, "the town Dad says has places to stay."

"How much farther?" Katie asks, honoring a routine we use on any trip.

"'Bout an hour," I say, per our script. Katie doesn't respond.

"Katie, don't be a wuss," says Jeff.

"Jeff, do you have any Clif bars left?" Katie asks.

"I brought one for each person, and I distributed them at lunch."

"Are you sure you don't have any more hidden somewhere?"

"No."

"Pretty please?"

Jeff is getting annoyed. My mom self wakes up.

"Katie, you've got a long history of resisting 'no' for an answer when it comes to treats. Do you remember your Thanksgiving strategy when you were little?"

"I want to hear about it only if it worked," she says, still with her eyes closed.

"We had family dinner at our house, and as people were saying good night, you asked for chocolate milk. I told you that it was too late to start a snack. After Grandma and Grandpa left, I hustled you kids upstairs to bed. You asked again for chocolate milk, and again I said 'no.' You nearly cried. Then you told me, 'Mommy, on Thanksgiving people say YES!' You got your chocolate milk."

Katie turns to Jeff and says, "This is your chance to turn today into Thanksgiving! Please?"

"Well –" He reaches into his pannier and hands Katie a Clif bar.

"Jeff, I am giving thanks for having the best brother in the whole world." As she bites into it she adds, "This chocolate mint Clif bar is the most delicious food I have ever tasted and will ever taste."

Not much later, in less than an hour, we cycle into the picturesque town of Uterga. It looks like a travel brochure advertising a Mediterranean haven. Its narrow, winding, uncrowded brick streets, whitewashed stucco buildings, tile roofs and effusive pink oleander seem like a movie set.

We stop by an arched doorway with a sign in Spanish: "Country House – beds." The price for the night is ten euros per bed. Double the money and you can also have dinner and breakfast. We say *sí* and *sí*. The brick entryway leads upstairs to a haphazard arrangement of rooms of varying sizes. We choose the largest room. It has four single beds, one in each corner. Other pilgrims would walk through the middle of our room to reach theirs. I don't think their noise is going to interrupt our slumbers.

At dinner, we try to chat with the four other pilgrims staying here tonight, but they speak German and little Spanish. The innkeeper's father, elderly Fernando, loves politics. He asks our opinion about George W. Bush, Bill Clinton and Monica, and he volunteers his. I feel chagrined that I don't even know the name of Spain's president. Fortunately he mentions it, so I don't have to ask. His daughter serves the meal – an iceberg lettuce salad, some kind of chicken stew, and a tray full of pastries. We help ourselves to wine. Joe chooses the red, and I the white. Knowing there is no age restriction on alcohol in Europe,

Jeff and Katie each pour a tiny amount of wine into their glasses. They give me quick glances, and I smile my approval.

As we finish dinner, Jeff says to Katie, "Let's get to know the locals."

"It's OK if you two go out," says Joe, "but be back here by dark."

When we rode in, I noticed a group of teenagers sitting in front of a café, and I suppose Jeff hopes to chat them up. How my son has matured! I'll never forget his question years ago when we were driving in San Jose one afternoon. From out of nowhere, my eight-year-old asked, "Mom, what's a condom?"

I glanced at his puzzled look and thought, "Here's my chance to give him a healthy attitude toward sexuality, or mess him up for life."

I launched into an explanation. His puzzlement grew. Finally, he said, "No, Mom. I saw a sign on that building back there. It said 'Deluxe Luxury Condoms.'"

So much for the Birds and the Bees.

As Joe and I wrap up our conversation with Fernando, we see Katie walking away from the *pension*, and Jeff riding his bike slowly next to her. He's wearing a brown plaid flannel shirt and cut-off tan Dickies, the likes of which kids in this village have probably never seen. Katie is wearing her blue Dickies and a red and white baseball shirt.

Joe and I go for a walk. We hardly feel the need for more exercise, but we're curious to explore this lovely town. We avoid the café to give the kids some space, and we stroll streets we did not see on our ride in. After we've walked for only a few minutes, the village morphs into the countryside. We pass fields, barns and warehouses. I hear "cooing," and a pair of collared doves flies from the ground up to a telephone wire. I take Joe's hand.

"Ducks in love," I say. We've always regretted that years ago we did not buy a painting by that name. It showed a pair of everyday ducks, not particularly beautiful, standing vertically as they touched their bills and breasts. I give Joe a quick kiss, and he puts his arm around me. We have stayed in love without that painting.

"Joe, we're approaching twenty-five years together!"

"With at least fifty more to go."

We stroll slowly. We are lulled by the calm evening, the wine, and the knowledge that we are safe in Uterga. We have a room at the inn.

I savor the mustiness emanating from the small, old, unpainted barns we pass. Dry alfalfa in storage sheds near the road resurrects sweet memories of my teenage summer days at the stable where I kept my horse. Is it because aromas are so non-rational, their associations so sensual, that they carry a power beyond the boundaries inherent in language?

The dusk deepens, and I suggest we turn back toward the village. On the way, I hear something strange.

"What's that weird babble?" I wonder aloud.

"The House of Commons," says Joe.

The sound seems to be coming from a large, corrugated metal building. It looks like the indoor ring where I used to ride my horse in the Rochester winter. A big door slides open for a moment, and we get a glimpse inside. Sheep and more sheep!

When we get back to the *pension*, we find Jeff and Katie are already there. They've changed into their pajamas, and they are brushing their teeth. When we crawl into our beds, none of us will have to count sheep in order to fall asleep.

Before turning off the light, I ask Jeff, "Did you find the locals?"

"Yes," he answers.

"And?" I pry.

"They liked my bike."

And then we are all asleep.

BUEN CAMINO

"Excuse us, on your left," I call out in Spanish as we approach a pair of pilgrims walking on the trail.

"*Buen Camino,*" they answer as they step aside.

"*Gracias, Buen Camino.*" We ride past them, and I realize that I've grown fond of this universal greeting that on the surface simply means, "Have a good trip."

The Camino, the trip, is very good this morning. The fog has cleared, and we're riding one behind the other on a tractor trail that wends its way across farms and fields. In the distance I just glimpsed one expanse that appears to be undulating like waves cresting in random whitecaps. Is this a mirage in the sunshine? The trail's rocks, ruts and weeds demand my attention, so I resist the temptation to raise my eyes again to look more closely at what I think I saw. But like Eve, I must know. I risk a quick glance. Ah-ha, the movement begins to make sense, partly because it also makes noise. The ringing of bells announces the approach of a herd of goats and sheep. We pedal near them, stop, and look.

Seen up close, the herd defies the image of a calm pastoral flock like the ones praised in romantic poetry. Some of the goats are playful, leaping when they could just as easily walk. The sheep vary in size. I bet I'm looking at Mama Bears, Papa Bears and Baby Bears, all dressed in sheep's clothing. The man who tends the flock could be

Merriam-Webster's illustration of the term "rustic." He's a couple of inches taller than Jeff, fair in complexion, and with a wiry build. He wears a big-brimmed, floppy brown hat, a tan shirt, drab green pants, and creased, dusty leather hiking boots. His staff looks like the ones in nativity scenes. As far as I can tell, the shepherd neither leads nor follows. He seems to be part of the current. Will our presence annoy him, a distracting intrusion in the herd's progress?

When he passes only a few yards from us, to my surprise, the shepherd neither sneers at nor ignores us interlopers. Instead, he strides over and gives a warm hello. His smile is genuine, but I'm taken aback by how few teeth he has. Based on every other aspect of his physical appearance, I suspect he's younger than Joe and I are, but were he a horse, he'd be judged way older. He has not had the benefit of my college's dental plan.

Joe is taping the scene, so I overcome my shyness and greet the shepherd. We chat about the weather, and then he asks where we are from. My accent and our appearance have marked us as obvious foreigners. I say, "We're from California." He responds in clear surprise, "Oh, that's very far away!" He may have no inkling where California is, perhaps an exotic land he's never heard of, or maybe he knows it's on the west coast of the United States. He is obviously amazed to be encountering us in his remote territory. Joe then joins the conversation, asking, "Is there a fountain near here?"

The shepherd says there is and gestures toward a junction of farm roads fifty yards ahead of us. We thank him and cycle to it, where we refill our water bottles and Camelbaks.

As we take turns, I say, "Kiddoes, did you notice that there were several black sheep in that herd? Do you know what the expression 'black sheep' means?"

"Sure," says Jeff. "It's the bad one."

"That's a very reasonable answer. All too often, 'black' is construed as negative in our culture. Can you think of examples?"

"Black Tuesday," says Joe. "When the Stock Market crashed.'

"Black mark on your name," says Katie.

"Who is the hero? The man who wears a black hat or a white hat?" I ask.

Neither Jeff or Katie responds. They have not grown up watching Saturday morning westerns on TV. Joe says, "I am a hero, and I wear a white hat."

"You are definitely a hero," I say. "But, Jeff and Katie, sometimes a black sheep becomes a hero. 'Black sheep' means the odd one out, the one who's different. In Japan, a proverb says, 'If the nail sticks up, hammer it down.' But as Americans, we appreciate the individual, the creative person who's different from all the rest. Kind of like us as biking pilgrims on the Camino."

"It's obvious that we're awesome," says Katie.

"Duh," I say, trying to match her style.

While we chat, Joe is studying the map he keeps in the clear sleeve velcroed on top of his handlebar bag. He says the next town, Azqueta, looks to be fairly good sized. He suggests we buy picnic supplies there. If this were 1984, I'd say that sounds double plus good to me.

The closer we get to Azqueta, the louder my stomach growls. We've ridden 35 miles since breakfast, and I understand how Jeff feels most of the time, which is more than ready to chow down, as he would say. I wonder if I'm going to end up talking like Jeff and Katie after being together 24/7. Will the influence be mutual?

We cycle into Azqueta, more of a hamlet than a town. Like all the others we've seen, it has a public fountain. This one is set into a large rock. The spigot is always on, and the water flows into a drainage basin the size of a trough for horses to drink from. I appreciate being able to carry small water bottles we can refill often and easily.

Like a water cooler that lures office workers to take a break and share the latest gossip, each town's fountain is the mecca for pilgrims. At this one, four pilgrims are sitting on two benches next to it. They are unwrapping sandwiches from what looks like commercial packaging. Joe asks them if they bought the sandwiches, and they explain they got them from the vending truck that just left. Just left? Yes, just left.

A local walks past us. Joe asks if the truck will return, and he is told that it comes only once a day. Joe then asks if there are any markets in town. No.

Another woman strolls past, and I repeat the question about any markets around here. She says there are none here, but there are several in nearby towns – off the Camino. What about the next town ahead on the Camino? Yes, she says, Los Arcos has a store. She adds encouragingly, "It's not far, only about fifteen kilometers." "Not far" in a car is pretty different from "not far" on a bike. But if the route stays fairly flat, and if the trail is smooth, we should be able to pedal that in a little over an hour.

"Let's search our panniers for any leftovers from yesterday," Joe suggests. "Even if they are stale, they can tide us over."

I pull out a quarter of a not-too hard baguette. Katie finds a not-too-bruised apple. Joe has a few squares of chocolate, and Jeff pulls out a box of peach nectar. We sit down under a big shade tree on a retaining wall at the corner of a yard and divvy up the dregs. It's hot at midday, and even the birds are quiet. I crunch into the bread but am surprised that the sound of my chewing is overpowered by the noise of a farm truck coming down the road. It seems out of place amid the small houses. It slows down and practically stops in front of us. Uh-oh, are we in trouble? Are we sitting on this farmer's property? What are the odds? He pulls into the driveway next to us and gets out. I imagine terrible scenarios in which he yells at us for trespassing.

I decide that if the woman speaks first the situation will be less confrontational, so I muster my assertiveness and say with a smile, "Thank you for the shade."

He smiles back. "Don't thank me. Thank the tree." He goes into his house.

"Everybody has been nice so far," says Jeff.

"I think that's part of the Camino tradition," I say. "Spain supports the pilgrimage as a mark of cultural pride. In the U.S., I bet there'd be a feeling of unease if a trail of strangers tromped from town to town."

"Especially if they looked as grimy as we do," says Katie.

I glance at my used-to-be-white socks.

"One of my favorite pieces of literature has to do with the pilgrimage tradition," I say. "Geoffrey Chaucer's 'Canterbury Tales.' One of his most famous characters, the Wife of Bath, brags to her fellow pilgrims en route to the shrine in Canterbury that she has also traveled to Santiago."

"Wife of Bath?" says Katie. "She obsessed over cleaning up?"

"She was from the English city of Bath."

"Tell us about her, Marty," says Joe.

"On her pilgrimage to Canterbury, the Wife tells a story about a knight who raped a maiden. He's hauled before the royal court to be sentenced to death for his crime. But the Queen gives him a second chance. He has a year to find the answer to a question. If he succeeds, his life will be spared. The question is one that Sigmund Freud asked more than five hundred years later: 'What do women want?'"

"What I want is lunch," says Katie.

"Me too. Let's start packing up while I finish the story. The knight travels far and wide, querying women and getting myriad answers: Women want money, beauty, flattery, love, clothes. None of these seems to be a ringer. Despondent on his 365th day, he comes across a raggedly dressed old crone. She says she will tell him what women want on the condition that he give her whatever she asks for if her answer proves to be correct.

When he gets to the Court, the Queen asks, 'What do women want?' and he gives the old woman's answer, 'Sovereignty.'

'That's right!' says the Queen. The loathly lady then demands that the knight make good on his promise. To his dismay, she wants him to marry her.

On their wedding night, he complains that she is so old and ugly. She says that she can become young and beautiful, but she will not promise her loyalty to him. Or, he can have her old, and she'll always be faithful. Which does he want?

The knight carefully answers, 'My wife, it is up to you to decide.'

"He was smart," says Jeff, "because the answer was to give the wife sovereignty, so he's letting her have what she wants."

"Bingo. She says, 'Now that I have sovereignty, you shall also have what you want. I will become young and beautiful, AND I shall always be faithful to you.'

Joe smiles and says, "You will always be young and beautiful to me."

"Let's go ridin'," says Jeff, hopping onto his bike.

"To Los Arcos," says Joe as we head out.

"The Arches," says Katie. "Do you think they'll have any golden ones?"

"I hope not."

Los Arcos exudes the ambience of a town that's been here a long time and knows it. We pedal on narrow brick streets between two-story buildings. Just as we had been told, we quickly spy a market. In fact, the market owner is so savvy she's got a gold plaque out front, "We stamp credentials." We pull out our credentials, little pamphlets we were given at our orientation that first evening in Roncesvalles. They are like passports on the Camino. Pilgrims can get them stamped at historic sites along the route to prove they have covered the miles and not just hopped a plane to Santiago.

I don't know how this shopkeeper got the right to be a credential stamper, but she takes her responsibility seriously. I have trouble writing the date. Spaniards put the day-month-year, in that order. The owner questions my credential because I put the 7 for July as the first number, and today is not the seventh. Joe helps straighten it out with her, and she finally gives me the stamp of approval. We buy two fresh baguettes, four cups of yogurt perfectly packaged with a little compartment of granola on top, triangles of soft cheese that Katie loves, and sliced mortadella that Joe orders in grams. I appreciate his fluency in Spain's system of weights and measures.

It's hot out, and we sit in the shade of a tree in a little park by the River Odrón. No one talks much as we inhale the food. And then, lunch is over. Many more hours of cycling await us.

"Before we hit the trail again, let's take a look inside that big church we rode past, only about a block back. I noticed a pretty rose garden next to it."

We ride up to the church of Santa María. I read from the guidebook, "'The church was built from the 12th to the 18th century.' I thought a lot of modern contractors were slow!" We enter the grounds through an open gate to the garden. Then we walk into the church itself.

"Unbelievable!" says Katie.

Having been to Europe several times and seen plenty of old cathedrals, I know the gold decorations, stained glass windows and statues in this one are not particularly remarkable. But this is the first ornate church the kids have ever seen. The virgins gape.

"It is beautiful, but I question spending money to create gaudiness instead of using it to help people in poverty," I say, kind of hating myself for tainting the kids' awe at what they're beholding. "I suppose a religious person could say that a grand church enriches the souls of the masses, but I think food in the belly does the job even better."

"I sure liked lunch," says Jeff.

"Ditto," says Katie.

We cycle out of this medieval town and pass a couple of pairs of pilgrims. We all say "*Buen Camino.*" We share camaraderie as we head in the same direction, but usually I am quite aware of our differences. They are almost all Spaniards, and almost all of them are walking. Many carry a traditional walking stick, about four or five feet long. A fairly common sight, though, is a pilgrim striding along with a ski pole in one hand, and a cell phone in the other. Even though July and August are the most popular months to make this trip, the route is not crowded. Every few miles, we see other pilgrims, usually alone or in pairs, but most of the time we ride by ourselves.

The Camino is organized into *etapas*, or stages. Each is the length of a rigorous but reasonable walk from town to town, usually between twenty and twenty-five miles. On bikes, we cover two or even three *etapas* per day, but we do not always go faster because of logistics for the four of us.

For instance, let's say it's 9:00 in the morning, we've been riding for a half hour, and Katie wants to shed her jacket. We all stop while she takes it off and stows it in her pannier. Walking pilgrims we passed earlier now walk past us. We hop back on our bikes and soon pass the walkers. Then the trail opens up to give a breathtaking view of a lush valley in the foreground and the ruins of a thousand-year-old church on a hilltop in the background. I am compelled to snap a picture. We all stop. Jeff says, gritting his teeth, "Hurry up, the walkers are catching up to us." But my camera and I are focused on the view. As soon as I've taken the picture, the smiles the kids have been trained to make on photographic demand immediately vanish. Jeff's face morphs into the picture of frustration as the walkers pass us. We mount our bikes, pass the walkers, and seem far ahead of them, when Joe stops to shoot video. That is never a quick stop. When he has finished, or given in to antsy family vibes, we take off again until Jeff needs to use a urination station, his name for any tree or shrub in the vicinity when he has to pee. So, four cyclists can be slower than a pair of walkers.

Our pace has been keeping steady with that of two women who started the same morning we did. We pass them, they pass us. After a few days of this, we greet each other like old friends. Unlike most pilgrims who look like mountaineers wearing baggy shorts and big backpacks, these women walk briskly, carry small packs, and they wear form-fitting shorts over their muscled legs. We nicknamed them the Spandex Ladies. In a town one evening when we were searching for a restaurant, we spotted the pair eating dinner at a sidewalk café. I said hello to them warmly, but they seemed not to know me. "Ah," I thought. "They don't recognize us in our civvies."

"I'm the astronaut on a bicycle," I said, in reference to my large white cycling helmet. Then they knew me immediately. For the first time, we introduced ourselves. Patricia lives in Andorra, and Ana in Spain. They met at a teachers' conference, struck up a friendship, walked the Camino together two years ago, and had so much fun they are walking it again. Our paths may continue to cross, or we may not bump into them again. Either way, I wish them a very *Buen Camino*. They inspired me to write the following after dinner:

The Spandex Ladies
for Ana and Patricia

*Con mochilas y sonrisas**
the Spandex Ladies prance,
walking westward with the holy
wearing stretchy, skin-tight pants.
Their leggy gait and buttock-binding
short shorts may enhance
their steady, daily progress

toward Santiago, far from France.
On bikes we speed right past them,
give a greeting and a glance.
We stop to rest and then behold
their cheeky buns advance.
We're the high-tech, bi-tech hares
on the ancient pilgrim trail.
The tortoises in Spandex
may be first to reach the grail.

* with backpacks and smiles

As part of our gear, we carry little radio/walkie-talkies that enable us to communicate with each other if we should get separated or if we simply want to relay a message without shouting. Generally staying in the rear, Joe captures as much as he can on videotape, riding one-handed with the camera propped on the other arm. When we lose sight of him, the kids have quit calling on the radio, "Dad, where are you and what are you doing?" We know he has stopped to take extended footage, and we might as well get our minds right about taking an extended break while we wait for him.

Jeff became familiar with radios like this when he was a counselor at Boy Scout camp last month. He taught the high ropes course, and I hate to imagine him letting go with one hand in order to send or take a call on the radio. I erase that picture from my imagination and instead smile at the memory of his offer to be the scout this morning. We usually have no trouble finding our way on the Camino thanks to yellow arrows painted on pavement and posts, or *conchas* (shells) painted on tiles set into the fronts of buildings. But in a little hamlet we couldn't find any. At a junction, we weren't sure which way to go. One way was flat, and the other climbed.

"The flat way must be the right way," I said.

"Mom's right," said Katie.

Joe pulled out his guidebook, but it didn't help.

"I'll ride to the top of the hill and take a look," said Jeff.

The rest of us took a breather while Jeff spun uphill, seemingly without any effort. He probably loved not being slowed down to our pace. He radioed back, "Summit intelligence reporting here. No arrows, no *conchas*."

"Well, come on back down then, and we'll take the alternative," said Joe.

Jeff wheelied back to us.

"Thanks for being our scout," I said. "Are you Lewis or Clark?"

"Yes," he said.

"Follow Pocahontas," said Katie, leading the way. I'm not sure if she knows how much more she resembles Sacagawea.

We are adjusting to our different moods and patterns. Joe wants to tape and not be hassled by our impatience. It's obvious that Jeff doesn't like to stop and wait, but he holds back his complaints. Instead, he and Katie trade intent looks, sometimes garnished with smirks of exaggerated suffering. As for me, I try to promote harmony. Early on, I instituted one routine that I credit to my father, a master in focusing on the positive. As we were loading our panniers on our bikes one morning, I said, "During a visit with Grandpa after he retired in Florida, I noticed that every day he commented appreciatively, 'It's another beautiful morning.' What would Grandpa Florida say right now?"

"It's another beautiful morning," the kids answered in

unison.

This exchange has become our daily mantra. Wherever we go, there we are. My dad is with us, too.

Buen Camino.

BIG EARS

Jeff is waiting for the rest of us at the top of a long paved ascent. I join him, and I am fuming.

"Did you see that group of Italian cyclists?" I ask him. "One of them was super rude."

"What happened?"

"Whenever I approach a climb, I work up as much speed as I can. I get a running start. Just now, I swooped past most of those guys. One of them looked totally winded, but as the rise began, he pedaled hard and just barely passed me. The moment he nudged in front of me, he slowed down. He slowed down! I had to brake on the uphill so that I didn't rear end him."

Jeff hears me out. I suspect he feels I complain too much about the difficulties of biking, all of it a piece of cake for him.

"What kind of bike was the bad dude riding?"

"He was on a road bike, heavily loaded with big panniers," I said.

"But what kind?" he persists.

Katie reaches us.

"It was the two-wheeled kind," she says.

From the top of the hill, we get our two-wheelers moving again. The pavement begins a gentle decline, and I reflect on what just happened. When Jeff looks at a bike, he sees it differently from the way most of us do – or don't. He notices the manufacturer, the model, the forks, suspension, frame, the material it's made of, the cranks, pedals, and only he knows what else. At age seventeen, he has begun to travel the same road in seeing a bike that Joe is well along in hearing a piece of music. Many listeners will say and truly mean "Oh, that's so pretty!" Joe may agree, but simply from hearing a piece, he can comment on the peculiarities or predictability of the melody, the harmony, the chord changes, and whether the rhythm is played on the beat, ahead of the beat, or behind the beat, as well as the mix, the timbre of the instruments, who played each one, and the name of the maker and model of each instrument played – all of this, just from listening with his big ears. Without training and experience, most listeners pay no attention to the elements within the music. They respond to the whole.

Jeff and Katie have always been surrounded by music. When Jeff was five and Katie four, they both said they wanted to play instruments like Joe and I did. Jeff asked for a cello like mine. We rented a one-fourth size for him. Jeff loved it until he discovered that most cellos are played most of the time by someone who is sitting still. When the cello was brand new, he constantly carried it around. I was baffled until I realized he was imitating what he had observed – Joe and me carrying instruments between the car and the house as we left and returned from gigs.

After Jeff was born, I stopped playing in nightclubs. I had been playing cello and singing in a duo with a singer/guitar player, but getting home at two a.m., and teaching a college class at nine a.m., didn't seem so do-able when I had a baby who needed me, too. After becoming a mom, I played gigs with Joe and other musicians on weekends, taking Jeff and then also Katie to stay with a wonderful family up the road. Joe and I generally played "casuals" – weddings, private parties, restaurant brunches and company picnics. Depending on the type of music we'd perform, we might leave the house looking like penguins (Joe in a tux, me in a black dress), or wearing party clothes or cowboy outfits. Whether we were going to play classical violin/cello duets or in western swing or bluegrass ensembles, we'd just put on the garb, load up the van, and drive to the gig

Katie asked for a violin like Joe's, and we rented her a 1/16 size instrument. She took to it effortlessly. Her fingers seemed to know where to go. She learned by the Suzuki method that emphasizes listening rather than reading, having fun rather than slogging through scales, and playing frequently with other kids.

At her first recital, she wore her favorite party dress, made of green velvet. Her white tights were tucked into her black patent leather Mary Jane shoes. At this musical debut, she didn't even play a piece. With four other Pre-Twinklers (not advanced enough to play the first tune, "Twinkle Twinkle Little Star"), Katie carried her tiny fiddle in the rest position under her right arm. She and the other little children lined up at the front of the stage. We parents stood right behind them for moral support. Taking their cue from their teacher, they lifted their violins and carefully put them under their chins. Then they bowed back and forth in rhythm to "Everybody Down Up." As a grand finale, they put their instruments back in rest position, bowed deeply, and then stood up straight and smiled. The audience went wild. I recall no on-stage moment when I've felt more proud.

We tried to honor Dr. Suzuki's maxim that you only have to practice on the days you eat. When Katie's practicing occasionally lagged, we used beans to encourage her. We put an empty jar on the piano by her violin case. Every time Katie played a minimum of ten minutes, we put a bean in the jar. When the jar was full, she could pick something special she wanted. One time she chose a radio, and another time an American Girl doll.

Jeff grew impatient sitting still holding his cello, and he stopped playing. But for Katie, music was almost always a positive experience. I envy her opportunity to learn the way she did. I wasn't allowed to start cello until I was in the fourth grade; Katie started violin at age four. In fact, when I was about four, I wanted to play piano like my mother and older sister did. I had eared out a few simple pieces that my sister played, and I decided I was ready for a lesson.

I don't remember what terrible thing my mother did one morning, but I knew my only response should be to run away. I grabbed my sister's music book, "Teaching Little Fingers How to Play," and walked to the piano teacher's house, about ten minutes away in our suburban neighborhood. I'd often been there with my mother. We'd wait in the dining room during Lynn's lesson.

I loved Mrs. Twitchell's front yard with its neat black lamppost by the curved sidewalk, lined with lilies of the valley. As I walked up it, I smiled at the flowers that reminded me of the song my sister's brownie troop sang about white coral bells. Feeling very independent, I knocked on the door as I'd observed my sister do. Mrs. Twitchell answered, and I explained I'd come for a lesson. What a grand lady she was. Instead of scolding me and sending me home, she welcomed me in and invited me to sit at the piano and play her something. I opened the book, which I couldn't read, and ran through one of the pieces I'd memorized. She told me to play it again, and she'd be right back. Although it didn't cross my mind at the time, I am sure she went to call my mother to tell her where I was. When Mrs. Twitchell returned, she did something I didn't expect. She showed me that I had a note wrong. How dare she? Then she said, "Do you know how to read yet? What grade are you in?"

When I said I was about to start kindergarten, she said she'd look forward to teaching me regular lessons after I had learned how to read. I walked home with mixed feelings. I was bored with the idea of running away because I really had no other place I wanted to go. I was proud I had had a lesson but impatient at having to wait for more. When I got home, my mother said, "Well, Martha, where have you been?"

"It was time for my piano lesson, so I went to Mrs. Twitchell's."

"What did she say?"

"She told me to come back when I can read. Will you show me how?"

Mom taught me how to read music before I learned to read Dick and Jane.

Katie has developed her music skills beyond classical violin. She expanded her interest to fiddling, acoustic guitar, and then electric guitar. When she took her first electric guitar lesson using Joe's vintage Fender Telecaster, her teacher asked with amazement, "How did you get Joe to let you take this instrument out of the house?"

"It was easy," Katie said. "I asked my mom."

She adapted her classical repertoire on violin to the Stratocaster we got her the next Christmas. Her version of the Bach Double Violin Concerto was electrifying with fuzz tone and distortion turned to the max.

To make music, she attends to the details of frets or fingerboards. But as for a bike, all she notices is its number of wheels.

Is the quality of experience lessened if we have the vocabulary and framework for analyzing it rather than responding only to the simple big picture? I believe it is enriched. I can't "un-know" that I'm hearing a cello play a melody, but my awareness that it's a cello does not detract from my appreciation of the sound. I imagine the instrument vibrating between my knees, the bow grabbing the strings, and the sound projecting outward to fill my ears one way and the ears of listeners another.

But at this moment my ears are filled with the sound of sparrows, our greeters at every village. The lane has deposited us onto a road leading into Santo Domingo de la Calzada. I don't see any cars or people. This part of Spain seems very little populated.

We cycle into the town, another picturesque assemblage of white stucco buildings with red tiled roofs. Flower boxes at street level boast red and white geraniums and bright yellow zinnias. We stop at a fountain in the center of a little plaza to refill our water bottles. Katie takes off her headphones.

"What are you listening to?" Jeff says.

"A mix CD that I made."

"What do you listen to the most?" I ask her.

"A Candlebox tune," she says and then laughs. "It's called 'Far Behind.'"

"Can I borrow your CD player in a little while?" asks Jeff. "Remember who gave you the Clif bar."

"Yes, Clif bar giver, you may use my CD player," she says, and she hands it to him.

"This town," says Joe, "is legendary."

"Yeah?" asks Jeff, stepping forward to top up his Camelbak.

"A pilgrim passing through here was accused of stealing. He swore he was innocent. They hanged him anyway, but he didn't die. People decided to tell the judge what had happened. When they told him, he was sitting down to a dinner of two roasted chickens. Not wanting to interrupt his meal, he said, 'If that pilgrim is truly innocent, these chickens will crow.'"

"And of course they did," says Katie.

"Of course. The young man was freed. To this day, a pair of chickens is kept in the cathedral here in Santo Domingo in honor of the miracle. Do you want to go see them?" asks Joe.

"I'd rather eat them," says Jeff

"We just had lunch!" I protest. "You remind me of Benny in 'The Box Car Children.'"

"I'm bigger and better looking," he says.

"Speaking of looking, everybody look up," says Joe.

We had not noticed that the monument right in front of us in the little plaza does not have the usual cross at its top. It has a rooster with a bright red comb, a black and white speckled body, yellow legs, and a purple, blue and white tail.

"Picture time, in front of the pyramid to poultry!" I say.

After the kids pose, Joe says, "Let's push ahead. We can stop for a snack in a while."

We resume rolling, as do my thoughts about how language affects the way we experience the world. I may be far from a classroom, but my English teacher self stays with me.

One of my professors at Stanford, writer Tillie Olson, lamented that she was "imprisoned in only one language." Before Jeff got his driver's license, I used to chauffeur him, Katie, and her friend Annie to high school every morning. En route, I taught a vocab word a day. I resolve to teach Jeff and Katie more language tidbits while we're here in Spain. The easiest time to share my pearls of wisdom was when the kids were captive in the back seat of the car. Now I've got the kids captive here on the Camino.

The friendly beep on my radio interrupts my planning. "I'm going to shoot this valley from the top," says Joe. I'm not surprised. The scene is exquisite. Although I'm huffing my way up a long hill on a not-too-smooth dirt road, the mown fields next to me draw my attention. They are golden and gorgeous. A giant orange thresher/mower is working in one, spraying clouds of dust, its droning engine the only sound on this hot, still afternoon. When the driver swings it around at the edge of the field, he smiles and waves at us. I wave back. Lining the road on each side are piles of rocks, many of which pilgrims have stacked into five-foot tall cairns. If the Wizard of Oz had included a stone man, these would be the archetype.

I reach the top, turn around and watch Katie pedaling toward me. What did it mean to her to say "yes" to this trip, which I think did not appeal to her at all? Is it that she was then 15, and still a child who went along with what her parents wanted? Maybe she considered the consequences of her saying right out, "I don't want to go." Maybe she didn't want to deal with the drama that might ensue, the guilt over her rejecting us, the burden of being the one who messed up the whole thing, refusing to be part of Team Kendall-Weed. Maybe it was just easier to say "yes."

Did she know her power? At what point do children recognize that they run everything? When Joe and I are tiptoeing around a parenting question, like will we let Jeff drive to a bike race by himself, or can Katie spend the night with a friend whose parents we think don't oversee their daughter's activities closely enough, he will say, "Who is in charge, us or the kids?" Good question, theoretically. But daily parenting seems closer to theater than theory.

If Katie were to say, "I like going on vacation, but I don't want to ride my bike an hour a day, much less fifty miles a day, and I will just stay with the McCrerys while you're gone," how would we have handled it?

Maybe she thought the trip might turn out to be fun, something to brag about, so her reluctance was an adolescent pose. What kind of self-respecting teenager will readily agree to being with parents 24/7, unless the offer is made to a bicycling fanatic like Jeff?

Or maybe she's still such a kid she didn't put much thought into it at all. Maybe while I was suffering angst about her attitude, it could be that at Manuel's Restaurant when she said "yes," she thought, "whatever," so she would be free to move onto more important issues, like whether she'd make Varsity soccer next year, what she should wear to the sleepover at Shannon's, or if the extra credit assignment in her history class would be worth the bother.

I can't even analyze why I do things, much less why Katie does. I am a human who wants to know why and how the world works, how people work, how my daughter works. But because I'm human, I'll never know. Motherhood is guilt and mystery and surprise and love so huge it dwarfs me. It is also this: My brave, sweating and lovely Katie is pedaling her bicycle up this hill like a girl who was born to ride.

Joe follows Katie. After he arrives, he leans his bike down and walks a few yards away to begin filming the landscape. The kids and I settle in to wait. We plop down on rounded boulders, a perfect classroom environment.

"Want to learn some Shawnee?" I ask.

Katie takes a sip from her Camelbak and says, "I was just thinking that's what I wanted to do."

"What are the other choices?" says Jeff, but his eyes show he's game.

"Here are two sentences in Shawnee: 'NEE la THAW wah KO tha' and "'NEE la THAW wah KO thite.' Hear the difference?"

"Only the last syllable," says Katie.

"Right. Now, here are the translations of those two almost identical sentences: 'Move the tree branch aside' and 'There's an extra toe on my foot.'" I hold up my left hand and with the right, move the left thumb down. "You see, the concepts are pretty similar. There's something solid, with something coming off to the side, whether it's a tree branch or a toe. For the speaker of Shawnee, it's easy to notice the parallels because the language builds them in. But English does not encourage us to see the similarity between tree branches and toes."

The kids are intrigued, so I continue.

"Here's another example of the way speakers of very different languages may understand the world. In Hopi, there are no subjects and verbs."

"Sweet," says Jeff.

"Instead of requiring that each sentence have a subject that 'does' a verb, Hopi organizes and describes phenomena in terms of concepts expressed in one indivisible linguistic unit. In that language, for example, if there's a flash of light, speakers say simply 'flashing,' whereas in English, we say 'something flashed.' How many aspects of the natural world have we missed or misunderstood because we try to frame them in subjects doing verbs? Some linguists suggest that our most creative scientists should learn a language that's really different from English, enabling them to have a new way of thinking about things.

In Kechua, an indigenous South American language, people speak of the past being spread out in front of them. Where do we say the past is?"

"It's behind us," says Jeff.

"And the future is ahead of us," says Katie.

"Right. When asked for clarification, the South Americans explain: 'We know what happened in the past, we can see it. But the future is unknown. It's hiding behind us.'

Jeff, when you were starting to talk, one time you walked around your bedroom and pointed to things, which I named. You pointed to a wall, and I said 'Wall.' You walked around the corner and pointed to another wall, and again I said 'Wall.' You were puzzled. You pointed to the next wall, and when I said 'wall' again, you got bored. You have always been very much in touch with location, and I think you felt those walls should have different names because they were in different places."

"English is not good enough for me," says Jeff.

"It sounds like no single language is good enough for anybody," says Katie.

"Someday we should learn a language besides Spanish, one that's not so similar to English. I think our vocabulary really affects what we notice. Take something as simple as the word 'water.' Some Native American languages use a different word for it depending on whether it's flowing in a river, coming in waves on an ocean beach, or sitting in a cup waiting to wash down some pemmican."

We each sip our water.

"During my month in Costa Rica, I learned that time does not always translate the same," Katie says. "Friends would say they'd come by at four o'clock, and if they were really punctual, I'd expect to see them about six."

"That's the way it was when I spent a summer in Mexico, when I was your age. I also discovered that I didn't know how to be polite."

"Please tell us," says Jeff in his politest voice.

"As my Spanish improved, I realized that fluency went beyond vocabulary. My American directness probably seemed insensitive. I learned that content often took second place to effusiveness."

"Excuse me?" says Jeff.

"Here's an example. A cousin brought over her new baby. I came up with all the words I knew for 'pretty,' 'cute' and 'charming,' almost a dozen of them. I felt like I was oohing and cooing right along with the other admirers. But my tribute was over way too fast. The other family members gushed far longer than I could, and I suspect I was perceived as uncaring and blunt. Sometimes it isn't just what you say, it's how much you say it."

"What was that story about your saying the wrong thing in Mexico?" asks Katie.

"Because Spanish and English derive from the same Indo-European language group, they share a lot of cognates, words with similar pronunciation, spelling and meaning. You already know that from your experience using Spanish. They give us a huge boost to our vocabulary. In Mexico, I would think of an English word, tack on a Spanish ending, cross my fingers, and speak right up. But one time that got me in trouble."

Katie giggles. Now she remembers how this goes.

Joe carries the camera to another tree that he leans against to steady his arm, and he's shooting again. I may as well tell the story, as we're not going anywhere for a while.

"I had done something I felt sorry about and decided to apologize to the family. Wanting to say, 'I'm embarrassed,' I said '*Estoy embarasada.*' They looked at me in horror. I didn't think what I had done was that bad, but they clearly did. Conversation got very touchy. Then I finally realized that *embarasada* does not mean 'embarrassed.' It means 'pregnant.' To this day I can't remember what I was apologizing for, and I bet they can't either. But I doubt any of us have forgotten that afternoon's failure to communicate."

"It's interesting that being pregnant seems to have the same root as 'embarrassed.' Being a functioning female is 'embarrassing,'" says Katie.

"What a good feminist you are! You are being generous in saying it's 'interesting,' When it comes to translations, I think misunderstandings may be most common not in translating from one language to another, but when people think they are speaking the same language, but they are not. For example, what do you kids want when you grow up?"

"I want to have my own truck," says Jeff.

"Can you think of any big picture goals?" I ask

"Well, I'd like to have a job that involves riding my bike, and I want to have a good family."

"I want to be a rock star," says Katie.

"I think Confucius said 'Choose a job you love, and you will never have to work a day in your life.' I think you will both find happiness and build good lives. The tricky part may come when you talk about the future with your potential spouses. They may think they share your dreams, but do they share the same definitions? A Harvard psychologist named Carol Gilligan says men and women speak different languages that they assume are the same. 'Marriage' and 'I love you' do not necessarily mean the same thing to a man and woman who believe they are in love and they want to marry."

"I'll settle for a girlfriend," says Jeff.

Joe joins us and says, "Sorry that took so long."

"No problem. I gave the kids a college lecture about language."

"What did you tell them?" he says.

"That I love you, and we agree on what it means to be happily married."

"Watch out, Jeff, they're going to kiss." So of course we do.

"Let's go ridin'," says Jeff.

As we pedal, I wonder if Jeff and Katie are thinking about what I just told them. Or is Jeff fantasizing about one of the girls in his English class. I've heard that teenage boys think of sex at least once every three minutes. Katie's thoughts may have drifted away from words to music, and maybe she's mentally in the middle of a Brandenburg concerto or a Steve Miller tune. We are in the same place at the same time, but we may be continents apart. At this moment, Joe might be reminiscing about his student days in Granada. The memories we are making will reveal more about each of us than the objective facts of our ride.

I'm reminded of a story that my father told me. He said that when I was a little girl, I mentioned at dinner that I remembered his going out every night as a member of Civil Defense during World War Two. Too old for the military, he contributed to the war effort by patrolling our neighborhood to be sure people had pulled their shades down. A potential bomber would not know the location of a city if lights did not give it away.

"It's so interesting you remember that," Dad said. I beamed with pride until he finished his sentence, "because you weren't born yet." I had heard the story so many times, I had incorporated it into my memory. I included myself in that memorized past. As Mark Twain said, "When I was young I could remember anything, whether it happened or not." Most memories we shape to suit us. This can be a good thing.

My dad often said, "Things have a way of working out for the best." He told me my mother questioned whether they should bring children into a world so terrible it had caused World War One, the Depression, and World War Two. He responded, "You can't go through life like that. You have to hope for a good future."

My parents were very thoughtful. When I was four, they built an addition on the house so my brother, sister and I could each have our own rooms. I felt it was incredibly generous of them to give us kids individual bedrooms, yet they still shared.

Ah, Mom.

I was a sophomore playing cello in the Tufts University orchestra. My instrument was called a "lady's" cello because it was slightly smaller than today's conventional size. It was a 1798 Hornsteiner. The scroll showed plugged holes where gears used to tune the strings before the more modern friction pegs were installed.

I don't remember the piece we were playing that evening, but the joy of making music, a big sound – the physical, emotional synergy – uplifted me as it always did. I relished the communing of spirits in ensemble playing. A girl from my dorm (we weren't yet calling ourselves "women") entered the rehearsal hall and waved to me. She looked uncomfortable. I finished playing the piece, lay my cello down by my chair, and walked over to her. She said the dorm mother had asked her to come get me, that I'd received a lot of phone calls, "something about your mother." I couldn't imagine what it might be, but walked back to the dorm.

The girl at the reception desk handed me a stack of little pink "You have a message" notes, the kind you tear off a gummed pad. I recognized the phone numbers on the first three – my house, my older brother's, my older sister's. I didn't recognize the fourth one.

In my dorm room, I called them, one by one. Nobody answered the first three, but when the fourth one picked up, I recognized my aunt's voice. She said, "Oh, Martha, I was hoping I wouldn't have to tell you."

My mother had died that afternoon. Her brother and father were both doctors, and they said the cause of death was a cerebral hemorrhage that occurred while she was taking an afternoon nap. She was fifty. The only thing my mother ever did wrong was to die so young.

A few months later, my uncle mentioned the cerebral hemorrhage my mother had when she was pregnant with me. I had not known. I asked my dad why he and Mom had never told me, and he said they had been afraid I might feel guilty. He explained that one night during her pregnancy, Mom woke him up and asked for a glass of water. When he returned with it, he found her unconscious. He called an ambulance. In his car, he followed it to the hospital. En route, the ambulance stalled. Dad pushed it with his car to get it restarted.

The doctors said she should not risk the strain of natural childbirth. Therefore, I was born by Caesarian section. Dear positive Dad told me, "We always thought you were such a good baby to make up for all the difficulties before you were born."

Dad was not a college-educated man, but he was wise. "If you want to have a good life," he said without saying so, "find a way to think of your life as good. Attitude is everything." William James put it this way: "Believe that life is worth living, and your belief will help create the fact."

The ring of my radio jolts me back to the present. I scramble to grab the radio from my handlebar bag without losing control of my steering.

"Hey Mom and Dad, how about a snack in this town?" Jeff asks.

Joe answers on his radio, "Sounds good. I might just have a little treat for us. Stop when you see some shade or a fountain."

This village is a triple winner, for it has a fountain and benches next to it, and they are in the shade.

We take turns filling our water bottles and Camelbaks.

Katie says, "I think we need handles for our radios."

"You mean to hold onto them?" I say, thinking of my awkwardness in pulling it from my bag.

"Mom, a 'handle' is a name. So you know who you're talking to."

"What handle do you want, Katie?" says Jeff.

5'2" Katie looks up at her brother and says, "I'll be Soaring Eagle. You can be Wounded Sparrow." We burst out laughing.

Joe stands and makes an exaggerated show of taking something from his pannier, but hiding it from us. Then, the Drama King holds out two oranges, a clump of grapes, and a red box. The box contains cookies that have become our favorites in spite of the name that we know would doom any sweet marketed in the U.S.: Digestive Biscuits.

"What's in a name?" I ask.

"'Digestive' means 'delicious,'" says Katie. That's how we'll always remember these cookies. As for how each of us will remember this ride, we'll have at least four different versions, all of them accurate.

WEED CLIP

Having lived with a Weed for most of my adult life, I've had firsthand experience observing people's reactions to a name that can be judged to be way cool or way embarrassing (that's not *embarasada*).

When Joe and I were first together and he was playing in night club bands, some of them supplied him with custom jackets inscribed with "Smokin' Joe Weed" or "Killer Weed." One heavy-toking blues singer took me aside and confessed, "I want to marry Joe and become Mrs. WEED." I've heard him called the Weed Man, and I admit I've whispered to him that he's a Weed Whacker. Our kids have grown, of course, like -----.

Name-related truth is stranger than fiction when it comes to my in-laws. A Weed married a Head. Fred Weed married Ruth Head, and they had four children, one of whom is my beloved Joe.

At this moment, my beloved Joe is standing at a crowded breakfast counter, a polished mahogany bar tended by a professional wearing a white shirt and black bowtie. Already the air is smoky, and china cups and plates clatter loudly in this high-ceilinged, tile-floored café. Liquor bottles line the shelf behind the counter, incongruous sepulchers of the night amid the white porcelain saucers of the morning. Joe is ordering for us. He knows what we want. Jeff and Katie like toast with jelly, and Joe and I get croissants. Joe orders plain coffee for himself, but the kids and I prefer *café con leche*, the Spanish equivalent of café au lait. At home I drink black coffee, but here I crave every extra bit of nutrition. Joe's coffee comes in a tiny cup. Mine is twice as large, and I savor every sip.

We're sitting at a little round table next to a plate glass window. A funky old motorcycle is parked just outside on the sidewalk. Perhaps that's what prompts Jeff to ask, "Dad, when did you do that motorcycle trip? Was it when you were a student in Granada?"

"It was later than that. About a year after I returned to San Jose State to finish my B.A., I got a letter from my friend Mike inviting me to come back over and help him with an article for *Cycle World.* It was to write about exploring the back country of Spain on off-road motorcycles."

"Sweet gig!" says Jeff.

"I thought so too. We did another article together too, but my name's not on it. It was for *Lookout*, a European travel magazine. We interviewed the director of a school for flamenco music in Morón de la Frontera."

"Flamingo?" says Jeff. I'm not sure if he's kidding.

"Flamenco is a traditional style of singing," says Joe. "After we finished both stories, I came back to the States. Mike sent me the letter he received from *Lookout.* The editor demanded to know Joe Weed's real name, one 'not so suggestive of drugs.' Mike vouched for me, but the editor would have none of it. When the article was published, Weed was nowhere in sight."

"Kiddoes, how do you feel about having Weed as part of your last name? Is it cool, or does the hyphen seem nerdy?"

"I've been Kendall-Weed all my life, so I'm used to

it," says Jeff.

"When I was little, kids used to call me Katie Wee-Wee."

"Katie Wee-Wee, I like that!" says Jeff.

The waiter brings the breakfast. Before I take my first sip of coffee, I hold up my cup and ask, "What would Grandpa Florida say?"

"It's another beautiful morning," responds Team Kendall-Weed in unison. We clink our cups.

After breakfast, Joe stands and says, "Whoever needs to use the bathroom, why don't you, and then let's head out." Katie Wee-Wee is the first to go. Bathrooms are a luxury on the Camino. We rarely see one between the time we have breakfast at a café and when we settle into a hotel very late in the day. I have no doubt that Spaniards have the same physical needs we do, but I don't know where they take care of them. Katie and I like pedaling any trail with nearby trees or shrubs. When nature calls, we like being surrounded by plenty of nature.

"Misty, misty, misty," I comment to Katie as we put our helmets on outside the café, gray skies overhead and dampness all around us. "I had no idea it would be so cool here. I should have brought long pants. All I have is my pajama bottoms, but they're way too flimsy for bike riding."

"I'd loan you my pants, Mom, but I don't think they'd fit," says Katie. She's two inches shorter than I am.

"Thanks, sweetie. Even if they did, I wouldn't take the shirt off your back or the pants off your bottom."

"I guess I'm wearing the pants in this family," says Katie, noticing that Jeff and Joe, as well as I, are wearing shorts.

"Speaking of pants, do you remember the story of

bloomers?" I say as we pedal slowly out of town on the bumpy cobblestone street, virtually free of traffic at this hour.

"I remember they're not flowers," says little Ms. Smug.

"Elizabeth Cady Stanton loved them. Imagine what it would be like to have one hand almost always occupied in lifting up a long skirt just so you could walk around, much less ride a bike. Elizabeth recognized the freedom that comes from wearing the pants in the family, in the town, in the world." My right hand's grand gesture as I conclude this oratory shows how much my cycling confidence has grown.

"Am I remembering that bloomers were named for Amelia Bloomer?" says Katie.

"Excellent! She supported reforms that she thought would strengthen the family, but not the radical demand for women's right to vote. She knew that if wives voted, the institution of marriage would be destroyed."

"Obviously," says Katie.

A storekeeper on our right is hosing the sidewalk in front of his shop. I pedal ahead of Katie so we can go single file past the spraying water. The streets remain generally empty – it's still early for most Spaniards – so after we're out of hose range, I ride slowly until Katie catches up. We are approaching the edge of town, and I can see green countryside not far ahead. The mist is already beginning to lift.

"Bloomer thought the new outfit seemed sensible for hard-working housewives and mothers, so she advertised it in her newsletter *The Lily*. You wouldn't believe the uproar. Harper's magazine said, 'We consider women's dresses to be more sacred than the Magna Carta.'"

"Is that more holy than the Gettysburg Ad*dress*?" says Katie.

"What's going on up there?" Joe broadcasts from his usual last-place position.

"Katie and I are appreciating our foremothers who started the movement that allows us freedom of movement."

"Great. Can you stop your movement when we come to a vineyard? I want to shoot some footage," Joe says.

"Roger that," says Jeff in the lead.

I intuit Jeff and Katie's response is the same as mine. Here we go again, more waiting for Dad. I know some day I'll appreciate having these videos, and the kids will too, so I try to be a grownup and restrain my impatience. Jeff, in the lead, dutifully stops at the top of the hill we were pedaling up. When he turns around to look back toward us, I am startled by his profile against the bright sky. My son looks like a man. His shoulders are broad compared to his waist, and his posture suggests masculine confidence. Thank goodness he has left the Jack in the Box styrofoam head tied on top of his helmet. Jeffy Joe still lives inside that expanding chest.

I catch up to him, followed by Katie and then Joe. I reach back to my pannier to pull out my water bottle. The moment my hand leaves the handlebars, they swivel, and the bike, now off-balance, falls under me. I drop the water bottle and grab the air where the handlebars used to be. The chain thumps into my right leg, smearing a patterned half moon of black grease on my calf. I hate this! But then my mother self, the angel over the right shoulder, flies into the picture. "Be a good role model. Show that frustration can be handled without resorting to vulgarities." While my id and superego battle it out, Jeff comments casually,

"Having grease all over your leg is the sign of an amateur."

This amateur is not pleased at being called an amateur.

Joe says as he holds the camera up, "We need a device that slides up and down the bike stem and prevents the handlebars from turning, kind of like a parking brake."

"Yes," I say. "A lightweight clip. Joe, we need a Weed clip!"

Our eyes meet, windows of our souls merged in the smoky '70s. We get the grins.

"Mom, until somebody invents that," says Katie, "let's go shopping for black cycling pants."

She surveys our surroundings, with no stores in sight. However, she can't help noting the stunning scene. "This valley is really pretty. The old, old buildings and narrow road don't look like California, but the natural scenery does."

"If I could draw anything other than a stick figure," I say, "I'd be setting up an easel. Look at these colors. The earth is dark purple, and the fields of yellow, green and brown look like a paint-by-number masterpiece."

"I love the vineyards," says Joe. "We're coming into La Rioja, the Napa Valley of Spain."

I look at the vineyard next to us, neat rows of gnarly vines bubbling over with plump fruit. "These clusters of grapes look like they're ready to burst. You can almost see them converting sunshine to sugar."

"That's what you do," says Joe.

"Let's go ridin'," says Jeff.

By the time we hop back on our bikes, the mist has fully burned off, and the morning temperature is perfect. Bright red poppies poke their life-affirming heads up on the margins of the lush fields. We cycle a fairly smooth dirt road that occasionally becomes a paved lane as it wends through towns every few miles. My legs rotate easily.

How lucky Katie and I are to be alive now, pedaling in this spectacular countryside without worrying about skirts or bloomers. Too few American girls realize how good we have it.

I wrote my first book for children because I was determined to bring some women's history to light. I had discovered the extent of my being in the dark when I was sitting in the front row of a history class at San Jose State University. I'd been teaching English at City College for a few years, and a Dean asked me if I'd like to teach a new course on Images of Women in Literature. "I sure would!" I answered without a second thought. When I got home, I had several second thoughts. What would I teach? That part was easy. I'd taken a course on Women in Lit at Stanford. But I felt insecure about my knowledge of the historical context for women in the literature.

I signed up at State for a course on Women in American History. As Professor Billie Jensen lectured, I took voluminous notes. I felt embarrassed that I knew virtually none of the material. Then my humiliation turned to anger. Why didn't I know information about women that was equivalent to what I'd learned about men when I was in the third or fourth grade? I resolved to write a book for kids about some inspiring woman they deserved to know about before they enrolled in graduate school.

Had I ever written a children's book? No. Had I read one since I was a kid myself? No. But ignorance is bliss, and I had the Zen of the beginner. I picked Elizabeth Cady Stanton as the person who deserved to be better known. I wrote the book and submitted it to numerous publishers. The few who responded with more than a form letter rejection offered a Catch 22: because nobody had ever heard of Elizabeth Cady Stanton, nobody would buy this book. At the time, I thought it took forever to find a publisher, but now I know that a year's search was lightning fast. The publisher was a family operation that specialized in New York State history.

Elizabeth Cady Stanton organized the first women's rights convention, in Seneca Falls, New York, in 1848. I've visited there many times, and I took Katie with me for the 150th anniversary celebration. Elizabeth demanded equality for women in every part of society. She raised seven children, and she looked like everybody's favorite grandmother with her tight white ringlets and voluminous lap. But as is true about the strengths of most people, you can't tell by looking. She wrote, "We hold these truths to be self-evident, that all men and women are created equal." So mind-bending for the time.

I thought *Elizabeth Cady Stanton* would be my one and only book, but after I quit playing in nightclubs, I started concocting more ideas for children's books.

During family dinner each night, Joe and the kids heard the achievements of whomever I was writing about – Nellie Bly, John James Audubon, Steve Wozniak, Jane Goodall, Ben Franklin, or Susan B. Anthony. Or we heard Joe tell about recording sessions in his studio.

Jeff and Katie talked about their days at school. Their stories prompted my first children's book on conflict resolution. It seemed to me that the problems they encountered were universal: how to cope with jealousy, cheating, bullies, secrets, the loss of a friend, or not making the team. I wrote a collection of stories about a character named Lisa and her older brother Nick. In each one, Lisa solves her problem, but Nick struggles with his. Because he's older, he deals with a more serious version of the same ethical dilemma. Before the story ends, I invite readers to make up their own ending. Kids control the outcome for Nick, and by extension, the outcome of their problems, too. I provide an ending in which Nick makes choices adults would encourage, and kids can compare their endings with the one I give. Nick was of course inspired by Jeff, and Katie is credited in the dedication as my co-author. She used to sit on my lap as I wrote. She'd do the reality checking as I composed the dialog. When she said, "Mom, no kid would ever say that," I'd revise until she gave her approval. Even now, when the kids are teenagers, I sometimes ask, "What would Nick and Lisa do?"

A lone car comes, and I scoot ahead so we can ride single file to let it pass. I think about my talented daughter cycling on the road twenty feet behind me. What will her future be on the road ahead? She says she is going to be a rock star, and she might if she gets lucky. She lacks nothing in musicianship, but that has nothing to do with success in the rock world.

Joe and I played a handful of concerts with the great mandolinist Tiny Moore, a veteran who toured and recorded with Bob Wills, Jethro Burns, Merle Travis and many other iconic musicians. Tiny's daughter talked about joining a traveling band, but knowing what the road was like, he wouldn't let her go. I hate to imagine Katie in the drug-filled world of too many rockers' lives.

Thanks to my generous husband, I have had the chance to record with artists far above my level of musicianship. I sing a little or play a bit of cello on almost every album Joe releases. I'm in the company of national stars in the acoustic music world. On Joe's last CD, "Swanee, The Music of Stephen Foster," I sang the chorus of "Camptown Ladies." Now it's stuck in my head, with a slight variation: "'Gonna ride all night, 'gonna ride all day. Bet my money on the Kendall-Weeds, who's 'gonna bet on the bay?" I slow my pace and wait for Katie to catch up to me. She rides her dark blue Trek, a smaller version of my white one, alongside me. I sing her the refrain, hoping she'll join in. She knows the tune well. She's fiddled it in concerts with Joe and me.

"Nice, Mom," she says.

How can she resist singing along? Duh, she's sixteen. If her reluctance to vocalize with me is our biggest communication problem, then I am more than a little lucky. Should I express my worries about a possible future for her as a rock and roller? No, I am going to encourage her to pursue her talents and trust that her good sense keeps her out of trouble. She can make a good ending for both Lisa and herself.

I confess I wish I could keep Katie close, protected from danger forever and ever. I hate the way a mother's job is to make herself unneeded, to make kids independent. Ever since Joe cut the umbilical cord at each baby's birth, I've struggled against mother-child separation. This trip as a foursome is likely to be our last. This thought socks me in the gut. Will I ever learn how to let go?

Did my mother worry about my future this much? Of course she did. I remember one afternoon near the end of my senior year of high school when we were riding in her green Buick Special. We had just left our house on Collingsworth Drive. I said, "I'm not really sure why I'm going to college next year when what I really want to do is train horses."

I was surprised when she didn't respond. Now, I get it. Her head and heart must have been reeling.

I loved riding and showing hunters and jumpers. My horse was not of championship caliber, but wealthy families asked me to exercise, train and show their horses for them. But even then, I knew that becoming a professional horsewoman would be fun for a while, but not satisfying for a lifetime. Still, I was testing my mother's reaction, which she withheld.

I also thought about becoming a professional cellist. I loved music, but spending hours playing classical pieces by myself in a tiny practice room didn't appeal to me.

After I enrolled at Stanford University, horses and music connected in an unexpected way. I had bought a young thoroughbred filly from a horseman I had worked for in Texas. I was training her at the Stanford stable with the hope not only of having a good time, but also turning a profit when she was ready to sell to some young rider eager to compete on a well-trained horse. One day when I was riding, a friend mentioned that she knew someone who was making a recording. She was looking for a cellist. Could she give her my name? I said sure. When I got the phone call, she described the project and said I could create my own parts for the tunes. I said, "Oh, I'm a classical player. If there's no written part for me to play, I wouldn't be able to do it."

"The music is written," she assured me.

At the studio, I found the parts were only minimally conceived, but I was able to play along. The band eventually invited me to join them. As I gained experience, I composed pieces and played more and more by ear. I amplified my cello and started singing. When that group split up, some of us formed an original rock band together, and that's when I met Joe. It was in June of 1977. Our band had rented a rehearsal studio in San Jose's East Side.

It looked like the other unkempt buildings in a neighborhood of small warehouses and Ma and Pa businesses. One notch above a garage band, mine had a place to practice that was heated and didn't smell like lawn mowers and oil changes.

We renamed our six-piece band every few months. I think we were "Thunder" when Joe came to meet us. We were trying to replace a violinist who lacked our commitment to original music, lots of practicing, and loyalty despite few gigs.

When Joe walked into our rehearsal studio, I was tuning my cello. I sat on my drum throne, a regal name for a portable, padded stool whose top swivels up and down. I glanced at the new violinist, but his back was toward me. What did I see? Long straight blond hair that hung down to his butt. My interest was aroused.

He plugged in his violin and easily played along with our tunes. But no one was ready to make a commitment on the spot. Music was serious business. That is, we took it seriously, but as for the "business" part, I knew to keep my day job.

The next Saturday I stopped in at a popular nightspot called The Grog 'n' Sirloin. The club featured small bands that played for a listening audience. I'd heard that a woman would be playing violin that night in a three-piece group, and I wanted to check her out in case Joe didn't join the band. Maybe she would be interested in thundering with us.

When I arrived, I saw that four people, not three, were playing. Joe Weed was "sitting in," a euphemism for contributing for part of the night, but without getting paid. The woman I'd gone to hear was playing, too. On the first break, I spoke with her briefly, but she had no interest in joining a rock band.

I stayed to hear and see more.

Joe's playing was masterful. He and I talked through the remaining breaks that the band took. I was charmed by this good musician who was interesting to talk to about subjects in addition to music. He had read books, he had lived in Spain, he was witty, and his blue eyes showed not only intelligence but also kindness. He explained that he and the other musicians playing in the club that night had recently toured in a larger ensemble, so they had a shared repertoire of fiddle tunes, originals, and acoustic roots music.

He also explained that after he returned from Spain and finished his Political Science degree at San Jose State, he did not apply to Law School as he had planned. Instead, he worked as a professional musician playing fiddle and guitar.

It was clear that Joe's musicianship and performance experience were way ahead of mine. It was also clear that I was very attracted to this guy.

All roads lead somewhere, and as Yogi Bera said, if you see a fork, take it. If I hadn't been a horsewoman, I might not have gotten the opportunity to discover that I could play cello in non-classical settings. And it would be extremely unlikely that I would have met and married Joe, or heard of the Camino, much less ridden a bike on it for hundreds of miles.

I glance down at my knees. They are pumping steadily (thank you, Amelia Bloomer) while my mind lurches from one thought to another. The one constant thread for all my interests is teaching. When I was five years old and playing school with neighborhood kids on my back porch, I was always the teacher. I have taught riding lessons and cello lessons, and my life's work is helping college students discover how literature can, as Robert Frost said, make them remember what they didn't know they knew.

What I know now is that the narrow road we've been cycling is merging into a four-lane highway. This must be the main route into Belorado, a large town that is today's destination. I don't want to deal with the dangers of riding in traffic, so I hope we can exit this highway soon. I spot a two-story hotel on our left. It looks like an old-fashioned truck stop.

On my radio, I broadcast to Team Kendall-Weed, "Let's check out that hotel on the left."

Joe radios back, "It's on the outskirts of town. Let's see what other options we have."

Here we go again. My perfectionist husband must consider every possible lodging before we make the life or death decision as to which place we'll sleep. Sigh.

"Joe, let's just give it a look. It's right here, we're here, and I'm tired."

"I agree with Mom," says Katie.

"OK, but I think it's not going to suit us." We park our bikes and go inside. Simply by the way Joe walks, I can sense his frustration about stopping here, a place he is determined to confirm is not right. With Elizabeth Cady Stanton on my mind, I am determined to participate 50/50 in this decision.

Judging by the handful of men hanging out in the lobby, with chagrin I must admit that "truck stop" wasn't far off. Joe asks if we can see a couple of rooms. The manager shows us. They are OK, but then he says they are $85 each. What? Last night we paid $36 for one room and $47 for another. And this place is six feet from a noisy highway.

"Well, I guess *this* time you were right," I say to Joe,

trying hard to smile. I put on my humility helmet, and we get back on our bikes.

We pedal into the center of town and spot a sign in the second-floor window of what looks like a fairly modern, three-story, boxy apartment building. The sign says that rooms are for rent on a nightly basis. It gives an address to get more information. We ask a pedestrian for directions and find the place, an auto repair shop. There, a man is working on a car, but when Joe asks about the *pension*, he introduces himself and explains that he does rent furnished apartments night by night. The kids and I wait by his shop while he drives Joe in his car to the apartments to take a look. When they return, Joe is smiling. He pays the charge, $21 for one one-bedroom apartment and $27 for the other. With the keys, we cycle back there together. The apartments are super nice, complete with TVs, radios, and living rooms. They are near the heart of town, but noise does not seem to be an issue. We're on the second floor, and the street seems quiet. The only vehicle that I can see is parked, and it's some kind of gigantic threshing machine. I try to imagine commuting in such a thing.

After showers, we head to the town square, an open plaza surrounded by sidewalk cafés. Even though we feel like we're at the end of a long day, for Spaniards, it's way too early to think about dinner, which is rarely served before 8:30 or 9:00. We have dubbed this time "the big wait."

"Let's get some *tapas*," says Joe. They are snacks available in the early evening, when I would like to devour dinner, but *tapas* are the only option. We sit down at one of the sidewalk cafés, almost empty at this hour. From the *tapas* menu we order drinks and a plate of toasted nuts and another of green olives.

Jeff inhales his share and then says, "I want to get to know the place. Maybe there are some other riders."

"Be back in an hour," says Joe. Jeff nods and zooms off while I struggle not to doze off.

To initiate conversation, I ask Katie if she has read anything good lately.

"*East of Eden*," she says. "I think it's my favorite book ever." I am stunned. Joe and I listen spellbound as Katie summarizes Steinbeck's classic and then considers interpretations of the symbolism. This girl is a born English major! Will she become a professor like me who plays music on the side but has a secure day job that she loves?

I wonder whether she will keep her last name all her life. If she pursues her musical identity, she might change it to sound more like a rock star. I bet she won't change it due to marriage.

Names matter, and I have kept my own. As for my husband, he's not your average Joe. I would love him just as much if he were Joe Reed, but it sure is fun to be married to Joe Weed.

MOOCHO POOSE

"My leg hurts," says Katie.

"Only your leg, you lucky thing? My whole body hurts. This is the most tired I've felt the whole trip, and I thought I could never be more tired than I was after the first day when we rode all the way to Pamplona." I flop down on the bed, one of a set of twins in this cozy hotel room. This is the first time we've found a suite that consists of two connected bedrooms and one bath. Up until now, we've always had to book two separate rooms, one for the kids and one for us. I don't know what families with small children do.

"Katie, why don't you take a good long shower, or even a bath? Soaking in warm water should help."

I hear her go into the bathroom.

The next thing I know, Joe is entering the room carrying little bags of crackers, green olives, almonds, and a half-size bottle of white wine.

"Ohmygod, I must have fallen asleep. I didn't even hear you go out."

"I wanted you to rest. You were beat."

"Thank you, thank you, thank you." How kind that he said "beat" instead of "bitchy." I feel guilty now for my impatience with Joe two hours ago. We had cycled into Burgos, the first big city since Pamplona. I was ready for the day's ride to be done, but Joe had to lead a search for the most perfectly situated, best priced lodging in the whole metropolis. He'd pedal up a steep street, then pull a U-turn, with us almost falling over doing slow-mo turnarounds, again and again. We circled the city's landmark cathedral, on a hillside, and went up and down side streets. The day's trek was lengthened by 45 minutes after we had "arrived" in Burgos.

Joe and I raise our glasses in a toast.

"To our first week on the Camino!" he says. We cross elbows and take a sip, a maneuver it's taken years to master.

"How would you describe the taste of this wine?" I ask Joe.

"Fresh and wet."

"Let's double check that." We sip again. The kids, with wet hair and clean faces, come into our room.

"Green crackers?" says Katie, furrowing her forehead as she tears open one of the snack packages. "They look weird enough to eat." I don't think Jeff even notices the color as he inhales the calories.

Every afternoon after I shower, deciding what to wear is easy. I put on the shirt I did not wear during the day. So, this evening I'll wear my blue shirt and wash my white one, whose color is becoming more like dusty ivory than snow. I also wash my socks in the sink, and then hang the wet clothes to dry overnight. I drape my cycling shorts on a chair pretending that they will air out, and put on my jeans shorts and the socks I did not wear when riding today. The boxy black case that serves as my handlebar bag becomes my purse, and I carry it with a long strap over my shoulder. I can't say my post-shower look is a transformation. I am what I am. Katie is wearing her red and white baseball shirt and blue Dickies pants, and she's pulled her hair into two braids. When Jeff packed, he wasn't concerned about weight, so he has carried the largest wardrobe. Tonight he's got on a dark green t-shirt and brown Dickies pants. Joe eschews cycling garb. His day-by-day rotation in shirts goes between a white dress shirt and a blue oxford cloth button down. The blue one is dripping next to my shirt in the bathroom, so now he's wearing the white one, whose color matches the darkening hue of my white shirt. He has put on blue jeans, which I wish I had brought. In towns, I never see anyone wearing shorts. By Spanish standards, we are casual weirdos in a culture that is much more formal, in dress and decorum, than we are accustomed to. Thanks to Spaniards' courtesy, and perhaps our smiles and fluency, no one so far has refused to serve us because of our odd appearance. I had thought we'd see people from all over Europe on the Camino and that we'd be anonymous in the international mix. Instead, with few exceptions, the pilgrims are virtually all Spanish.

When we go out for dinner, we already know that there are lots of cafés to choose from. We saw them all when we toured the city. I don't care where we eat, as long as it's close. The kids like a little spot with stairs going down into it, so we go in. It's smoky, of course. Smokers are welcomed everywhere, unlike in California where there's no smoking indoors at all, much less in restaurants. We do our best to ignore the yucky air so we can focus on the sustenance we've come for.

"This restaurant also has a *menu del día*," I comment as we peruse our menus.

"It has to," says Joe. "There's a national policy that all restaurants have to offer at least one choice of an inexpensive meal."

It is an amazing bargain, typically costing only ten to twelve dollars. This evening, as usual, that's what we each order. It begins with salad made of iceberg lettuce, long slices of yellow onion, a few spears of blanched asparagus, a large glop of tuna, and tonight, there's also a hard-boiled egg. The main course is roasted meat, from what animal I can not tell. Fried potatoes, not called "french fries," are also standard. Small hard rolls are served in a basket, and we can drink all we want of milk, water, soda, red wine or white wine. Dessert is a slice of melon.

At home, conversation stretches our meal times out, and I love to dawdle when we're together and relaxed. Here on the Camino, our dinners go as fast as the service allows. We are exhausted, we are hungry, and we eat. During the main course, though, Joe gets everybody's full attention when he says, "Burgos has a lot of sights to see. What if we stay here for two nights? I figured we wouldn't ride all day every day, so we have plenty of time."

I am startled by this unexpected suggestion.

"Dad, we should," says Jeff. "After a week's ride, we need a day of rest."

"Jeff, I'm amazed to hear you talk about resting," I say. "You're probably the one who is the least tired."

"Athletes always include recovery time in their training schedule."

"This athlete is ready to recover," says Katie. "Let's sleep in tomorrow morning. No more pre-dawn wake-up, OK?"

"Honey, we haven't been getting up much before 7:30, which is post dawn. But there's no need to get up early tomorrow."

We stroll slowly back to our hotel, anticipating a night of sleep that lasts not until the alarm clock rings, but until we are rested enough to awaken naturally.

But in the morning, Katie wakes up earlier than I do.

She doesn't complain about the hour. Instead, she complains about her leg. There's a sore spot on her thigh.

"I bet spending a day when you're not in the saddle will help," I say encouragingly. Then she shows it to me. It's a lump on the inside of her thigh, almost like an infected insect bite. She needs medical treatment. I'm glad we're in a city where it should be available.

The hotel concierge gives us directions to a medical clinic. The four of us pedal over, an easy twenty-minute, single-file jaunt in traffic that is not too terrifying. We wait only a few minutes, and then Katie is admitted to see a doctor.

I go in with her for linguistic and emotional support. The doctor looks at the swelling and says that it is a common ailment, an infected hair follicle. We explain that we've been riding our bikes on the Camino. The doctor says the sweat, and the rubbing of Katie's thigh against the bike seat, probably caused the problem. She will lance it and let it drain. The doctor pokes and cuts, and Katie grimaces. I do my best to keep my feelings under control. I get woozy whenever someone I love is hurt.

As the doctor works, she comments, "*Mucho Pus*," pronounced "moocho poose" (rhymes with "loose"). Granted, "pus" in English is not pleasant, but just think about having "moocho poose." Yuck. You can hear it "poosing." Brave Katie! But then she cries out, a quick yelp of pain.

"You've got to be brave, or else I'll faint," I say. She knows I'm only partly kidding, and she toughs it out. While the doctor applies a bandage, my mind drifts to word associations in Spanish beyond "poose" and "pus." On the positive side, I think *la luna* sounds more romantic than "moon," which makes me think of a fat cow bellowing while jumping over a chunk of cheese. Connotations reflect and create attitudes. "Scintillating" and "tipsy" might be two different people's descriptions of the same partygoer.

After we fill the prescription for antibiotics at a nearby pharmacy, Katie sits at an angle on her seat so the bandage doesn't rub as she pedals. We drop off our bikes at the hotel and refamiliarize our legs with walking rather than spinning.

The city's landmark gothic cathedral buzzes with tourists. It makes the old church the kids marveled at in Los Arcos seem Spartan compared to this elaborate display. Nothing exceeds like excess. In less than an hour, we have had our fill of stained glass windows, ornate carvings, and gold busts of people we don't recognize. Granted, what we deem "garish," another may call "gorgeous." We leave the cathedral and explore the neighborhoods.

We sample a couple of bakeries, stroll a statue-filled public park, and make a donation to a classical string trio practicing with their cases open for tips. We happen upon an arts and crafts fair similar to ones in California. Paintings, photographs, ceramics and macramé are displayed under pop-up tents. The vendors and their potential buyers look prosperous and almost universally Caucasian in contrast to the diverse residents of metropolitan San Jose. Most of the women are wearing dresses, and red leather shoes and matching purses seem to be the fashion of the moment. A few young couples are sporting jeans and American style t-shirts with phrases in English that don't make sense, like "Kitten Fuel" or "Alligator Is Magic."

In my right pannier I've been carrying a paperback

book, *The Prize Winner of Defiance, Ohio: How My Mother Raised Ten Kids on 25 Words or Less,* by Terry Ryan. Joe's mom gave it to us, and Katie read it on the plane. I started it when she was done, but we landed before I could finish it. I have been too exhausted after each day's ride to even think about reading it. Here in Burgos, I have finished the book. Its setting takes me back to my childhood in the 1950's. I want to give it to my sister, whom I know will love it, too. Mailing it may cost more than buying another book, but it feels right to send this copy to her, passed from family member to family member. We search out a post office to do the deed. When we find one and go inside, a constantly changing electronic signboard announces which clerks the patrons should go to, depending on their postal needs.

"This is more high-tech than in Silicon Valley," I say to Joe.

A young woman ahead of us in line turns to look at me. She says in English, "Are you Americans?"

"Yes!" I answer in complete surprise.

"I am too," she says.

"Why do you happen to be here?" I ask.

"I'm walking the Camino," she says. "I'm mailing stuff home that I don't need to carry."

"That's exactly what we're doing." She and I are identical except for a few details – she's young, blonde, tall and athletically slender. We become so engrossed in conversation that I miss the signboard's direction that I should go to window #4.

She says that she's been living in Germany where she's been employed in her profession as a ballerina. She stands straight, her right foot at a 45-degree angle from her left. Her arms gesture as she speaks, gracefully arcing away from her bosom. She explains that the production she last performed in finished its run, and she has chosen to walk the Camino, she says, "to clear myself out, to replenish my soul."

I feel the pressure from postal patrons behind us to move forward, and I go to my assigned window. When I finish mailing the book, I look around. The ballerina is gone. Joe and the kids are waiting for me in the lobby.

We walk outside, and I say to Joe, "We've seen our first American! But talking to her reminds me how strange we are, or at least I am. Unlike her, I don't feel like I have to clear myself out. Is there something wrong with me because I don't know what's wrong with me? Deep down inside, am I shallow?"

Joe laughs. "You're worried because you don't have anything to worry about." He puts his arm around me

Katie says, "Watch out Jeff, I think they're going to kiss."

We do.

I turn to the kids, "We are so lucky to be healthy, to have each other, and this adventure together."

Then I look at Joe, "How many miles have we ridden so far?" Joe tracks our progress on his bike's odometer.

"Almost two hundred."

I know how many we have to go, because markers on the Camino regularly announce the kilometers remaining to Santiago. From Burgos, it's about 450, or roughly 300 miles. It's way too soon to count chickens. As for the ballerina, I hope our paths cross again. If they don't, I wish her a *Buen Camino.*

The next day, antsy to get out of the city and explore the unknown that lies to the west, we get back on the trail. Katie wears her long pants to add another layer of padding over her lanced infection. She says she feels comfortable on her bike. Quickly the countryside engulfs us. The hills roll gently, and the ridin' is easy. I feel good except that I have "mucho poose" stuck in my brain. I think about students whose lives have had "mucho poose."

San Jose City College, where I teach, attracts a wide range of people. Some are retired professionals who have always wanted to take a literature class. Others are high-achieving 18-year-olds whose parents can't afford to send them to a private university. Low-income immigrants, eager to improve their English, come to gain a foothold on the economic mobility ladder. Employed parents struggle to complete a degree class by class, year by year. A handful come because it is a condition of their parole. Others are immature young adults unsure of who they are and what they want. Every semester, a few students give me the privilege of serving as a catalyst in their transformation from feeling lost or downtrodden to becoming self-directed and determined. I help them onto a perch, and from there, they take flight.

Funny how Joe and I mesh so well, yet his creative pleasure comes from making exquisitely beautiful music. He loves to spend hours tweaking a mix in the studio, perfecting each note, each phrase, each harmony. No matter that few listeners can appreciate the subtleties. He can. My work is validated not by what I do, but by its impact on others.

One student in my World Literature class a few semesters ago had had "mucho poose." Vicente moved to San Jose to escape the Los Angeles barrio where he grew up. He wanted to leave gang life, but he knew he couldn't simply resign and expect to be given a gold watch. His younger brother was already in jail, and Vicente wanted to have a different future. He begged a piece of cement floor to sleep on in the basement of his uncle's little house in San Jose, and enrolled at San Jose City College.

His first day in my World Literature class, he said little, and what he did say, I did not understand. His Latino gang-ese made Ebonics seem like the Queen's English. I am used to imagining final consonants that Vietnamese students do not pronounce, and I'm accustomed to the accent typical of Spanish speakers. But I had not heard enough of the L.A. gang idiom to make the necessary translation. And beyond words – his body language! His left hand covered his mouth when he spoke, and his right hand bobbed, with the first finger and pinky extended.

As weeks passed, I noticed that Vicente scored well on the daily quizzes. Apparently he was completing the reading assignments. He hid in the back row, but he did seem to pay attention in class. He gradually contributed more to the discussion; in fact, when I could understand his comments – offered in a soft, shy voice – I realized that he had good insights about the literature we were studying. By mid-semester, his style had changed. He moved his hand away from his mouth, and I understood more of his speech. His arm stopped bobbing. One choice on the midterm was to write a sonnet. He wrote one to his brother in jail.

When Vicente graduated from City College, he received a scholarship to the University of California at Berkeley, as an English major.

A friend used to say, "You're not responsible for the shit thrown at you, only for how well you duck."

My radio's cheery little ring interrupts my thoughts as we pedal into another picturesque village. As in most of the towns along the Camino, bright red geraniums in window boxes decorate the white stucco walls of the houses lining the narrow streets. Cars are few, and they are small. A pair of women carrying plastic sacks of groceries walk with their children who glance with curiosity at us, our American helmets and mountain bikes. The ubiquitous sparrows chirp, and a few old men seated under a shade tree nod as we pass. Joe broadcasts to us, "Let's get lunch supplies here."

Like a flock of birds that has communicated its flight pattern to all its members, we swoop to the next block's *Mercado Diana.* We lean our bikes against the store's outside wall, remove our helmets, and walk into the tiny shop. It offers the usual assortment of huge blocks of cheese, sausages, cured ham, fresh loaves of bread, Swiss chocolate bars, Danish yogurt cups, apples, oranges, and boxed milk and juice.

"*Muy buenas*," says Joe, greeting the proprietor. He begins the picnic purchase, loving every minute of the exchange. But you can discuss mortadella options for only so long, and finally we leave the store. I carry the baguette in my pannier, Katie volunteers for the apples and chocolate, Joe takes the meat and cheese, and Jeff carries the drinks.

We agree to pedal until we find a shady spot for lunch. As I am putting my helmet back on, I ask Katie, "How's your leg feeling?"

"It's OK. I notice the bandage, but if I ride carefully, it doesn't bother me."

"Great, honey. You're being a really good sport, and like always, a daughter who's easy to love." I give her a hug, normally a routine gesture made awkward because our helmet visors get in the way.

"I remember a Halloween night years ago when we

trick or treated with some of your friends. I was struck by how kind you were to one of the girls who was the odd one out, ignored by the kids who were too cool to be nice to her. When I tucked you in bed, I said, 'Katie, I am really proud of you. You're one in a million.' Struggling to come up with something to say, you took a while to answer. Then, with gusto, you said, 'Mom, you're ten out of zero.'"

"You still are, Mom!"

"You too!"

"Are you going to cry?" (She's known me all her life.)

"Maybe snurgle a little."

As we pedal off, I recall when Katie snurgled. In eighth grade, she won the Silver Quill Writer's Contest at her Middle School. The assignment had been to "write a letter to someone you admire," and she wrote to Melba Patillo Beals. Katie had just read Beals' memoir, *Warriors Don't Cry*, about her experience as one of nine African-American kids who integrated Little Rock Central High School in the 1950s. A year after Katie won the award, I was invited to speak about my children's books at a convention in Santa Clara. Each author was also asked to eat lunch at assigned tables and interact with conference attendees. When I saw that Melba Beals was listed as the keynote speaker after lunch, I asked the organizers if she and I could be assigned to luncheon tables next to each other. I brought Katie to the conference with me. When the luncheon ended, Katie and I left our table and approached Melba Beals. I introduced ourselves to her. Katie had brought the plaque she had won to show Melba, and Katie delivered the letter she had written her.

After lunch, Melba disappeared, returning about ten minutes late for her keynote speech. As we waited, I told Katie, "I bet she's hiding in a stall in the women's bathroom, taking notes from your letter."

"No she isn't!" said Katie, clearly embarrassed.

Katie may have been right that Melba wasn't in the ladies' room, but I had predicted accurately. During her speech, Melba read excerpts from Katie's letter. My eyes welled up with tears. I looked at Katie, and her cheeks were wet.

"Why are you crying?" I whispered as I passed her a kleenex from my purse.

"I can't believe a great writer like her is actually using *my* words, and I'm crying because I can't help it. I'm your daughter."

We resume riding in what has become our usual order, with Jeff first, then me, then Katie, then Joe. The terrain is easy. On auto-pedal, I resume my reflections about students who have dealt with "mucho poose."

Nawuth (NA-wooth) Keat was one of them. He seemed like many of my Southeast Asian students. He was attentive but quiet in my World Lit class, a different semester from Vicente's. When I presented the list of international books to choose from for the book review, he asked me to recommend one for him. Knowing he was from Cambodia, I suggested he might be interested in Teeda Butt Mam's *To Destroy You Is No Loss*, which describes one family's horrific suffering after the Khmer Rouge's takeover of the country in the mid-1970s. I warned him, however, that a Cambodian student a previous semester had selected that book but ended up reviewing another one because of the awful memories it resurrected. Nawuth nodded.

When Nawuth turned in his paper, I noted that he had read Teeda Butt Mam's book. He commented quietly to me, "Compared to my family, she didn't have it so bad." I was aghast. In that book, the cruel thugs who overtook the country bragged to their victims that each of them mattered no more than a single grain of rice. If a bowl full of rice was reduced by one grain, it was no great loss. I could not imagine the suffering Nawuth must have endured if his family had fared worse than the one described in the book. On the last day of the semester, when students were having a potluck and poetry reading, he told the group, "I'd like to share my story with you."

He said that he was nine years old when Khmer Rouge guerillas shot and killed his mother and infant sister, his aunt, uncle and babysitter. Nawuth was hit by three bullets. When a Khmer Rouge kicked him to see if he was dead, Nawuth purposely lay limp in the ditch that had filled with his family's blood.

"I'm lucky," Nawuth said. "I survived."

During the Khmer Rouge reign of terror, Nawuth worked in the rice fields as a child slave. There were no holidays, no days off. In spite of all the labor, not enough food was grown in the disorganized, inefficient system the Khmer Rouge controlled by guns, not good sense. Starvation killed more people than bullets did. All food had to go into the common pot, but when Nawuth went to eat, he was told the food was gone. To survive, he caught fish and eels with his hands. He trapped and ate monkeys, birds, rats, and snakes.

Nawuth escaped with his older brother, sister, her husband and their baby. They walked barefoot across Cambodia, dodging bullets and tiptoeing on trails lined with land mines. After waiting in crowded Thai refugee camps more than two years, Nawuth was sent by himself to the U.S. The rest of his family had been sponsored in

France.

As Nawuth told his horrific story, I looked around the room. I was not the only listener moved to tears. I said to Nawuth, whose English was rough, "Would you like me to write your story down for you?"

He seemed as surprised by my offer as I was. "Yes," he answered simply. I've been meeting with him regularly ever since. With courage, he dredges up memories that take him back to his painful past. The manuscript is a work in progress.

The Khmer Rouge takeover prevented Nawuth from going to school in Cambodia after the fourth grade. When he learned in his refugee camp that he would be going to America, he didn't even know where that was. On the airplane to the United States, many of the refugees found the American food they were served to be inedible. After enduring years of hunger, Nawuth ate. In fact, he ate every ham sandwich that others refused. He said he'd never tasted anything as good as the strange and colorful collection of sweets they were also served, which he later learned was canned fruit cocktail. He arrived at the San Francisco Airport, where he slept on the floor next to a "sculpture," a large trash can. At the barracks where the refugees were housed for a few days, he was the only one who figured out the hot/cold handles in the shower. But he did not know to turn on the heater in his room. In Cambodia, there is no need for heaters, and in his village, there was no electricity. He did not complain about the cold. He appreciated the used jacket he was given, and wore it all day and night.

Nawuth was placed in Oregon where he earned his high school diploma in just three years. He supported himself by working as a dishwasher.

Now, Nawuth is married and the father of three. He and his wife have bought a bagel shop. Nawuth also works in a machine shop. His children are tall, healthy, and fully engaged in the American pursuit of happiness.

My American family is now fully engaged in our pursuit of happiness. We're pedaling, sweating, and sometimes breathing really hard ("sucking air," Jeff calls it). We chose to do this. I'm reminded of a student who understood "choice" more profoundly than I expect – and hope – we ever will.

He was from Vietnam. Tien told me about his escape after the Communists took over in 1975. He and his best friend decided to pool their finances, buy a boat, and head out to sea with their two families together. Tien gave his money to his friend to get the boat, but he never saw the friend again. Not about to give up, Tien got his hands on a book that explained how to build a boat, something he had never done. Working in an abandoned shed, he managed to build a boat without being detected. He pulled the boat into the water and loaded his family onto it.

He explained that he thought they would have a 50/50 chance. They might be murdered by pirates, get washed overboard in a storm, starve from too many days adrift at sea – or they might be rescued.

I asked, "With odds like that, how could you risk not only your own life, but your whole family?"

He said, "When there is no freedom, there is no reason to live."

"Despair" derives from an Old French word meaning "without hope." Freedom does not eliminate "poose," but it offers the liberating notion that we do have choices, and there is hope. Western culture demands, "If you don't like it, change it." Some people say that God chuckles while humans make plans. Perhaps we have only the illusion of control over our lives, but that may be enough to provide the impetus to live at all.

My radio rings, and Jeff says, "I'm hungry." His statement of need that he assumes will be met is good and simple. We ride into another town where empty benches line the plaza in front of the public fountain. A few small trees provide shade. Again, our flock swoops in unison. We pull our picnic from our panniers and begin the pleasant, serious, and life-affirming business of eating lunch. I relish our privilege, so far, of having the means to cope with the very little "poose" we've had to deal with.

RULES RULE

On the edge of this deserted road, Joe is videotaping a patch of thick yellow daisies interspersed with blue cornflowers. The Spanish countryside seems to be Mother Nature's favorite child. Then I think not of the landscape, but its filmer.

"You are always doing the taping. You should be in a shot. Why don't you ride ahead, and I'll tape you."

Joe lifts the camera from around his neck and over his head, and puts it over mine. The thing hadn't seemed so huge when Joe carried it.

"Just do a loop, OK? Come back and get the camera. I don't dare try to ride with this weight hanging on me."

"Go for it," says Jeff, "on my bike."

Joe and Jeff switch bikes. I hold up the camera, which is surprisingly heavy to support for an extended time. Joe pedals off, and Jeff says as we watch him go, "My bike weighs twenty pounds more than Dad's."

"Why?" I ask, hoping I'm not jiggling the camera when I speak. "I thought yours was more high tech and therefore lighter."

"I'm carrying all the tools."

Joe is riding smoothly, so I zoom in on him. I do it way too fast. I imagine all of us getting nauseous when we watch this footage, maybe with the kids commenting that

Mom's found a way for us to experience the Tea Cups ride at Disneyland in our very own living room.

Joe turns around to come back to us, and as luck would not have it, two cars come down the road, one in each direction. Their engines break the quiet we have grown accustomed to.

"This place has turned into a freeway," says Jeff. The cars swoop around Joe, and when he returns, I am more than happy to relinquish the camera.

"How'd you like my bike?" asks Jeff.

"Not bad, for a kid's," Joe says with a smile.

My heart is full in this sun-washed countryside that's so picture perfect no picture could capture it. We cycle past a sign for a town called Matajudios, which could be translated as "Jew Killer" or "Kill the Jews." Santiago himself is known as *Matamoros*, "Moor Killer." Modern pressures for political correctness have not swayed Spaniards to revise these historic names. What a contrast between the bounty of this flourishing earth and the human slaughters that have stained it.

I savor my heightened sense of aliveness in this vibrant setting. My legs and lungs are working hard. My fingers sometimes tingle from the constant pressure on my handlebars, but I am feeling it all, right here and right now. John Muir said, "You can't waste time without injuring eternity." Songwriter Chuck McCabe wrote, "Life is short, and then it ends." I vow to make the most of every moment.

After my mother died, I was enraged at the unfairness that I could listen to a song she loved, *Love Is Blue*, but she could not. She could no longer play her lighthearted *Le Secret* on piano, the tune that signaled my brother, sister and me to get a move on, that Mom was waiting for us to gather our things and head out the door. She could no more read a mystery, comfy and relaxed in her blue overstuffed chair in the living room, with her freshly baked chocolate chip cookies cooling on the kitchen counter, ready for us when we got home from school.

I can picture her kneeling in that blue chair, waving to Dad through the window as he backed his car out the driveway on his way to work. Then she'd hurry to the window behind *his* chair and wave to him again.

My grandmother and mother talked on the phone every afternoon. How did my grandmother endure life after my mother died?

I wrench my mind from the past. I'll take a lesson from Jeff, who found his own way to increase his pleasure in the moment. A few days ago, Joe and I cycled side by side up a short but very steep rise on dark red clay between recently harvested hayfields. Joe wanted us to get ahead of the kids so he could film them from the front. At the top of the hill, we turned around and watched Jeff, who was right behind us. I was surprised to see that he was struggling, standing up on his pedals as he slowly pumped his way up. Joe said to me, "I bet his shifter is broken."

As Jeff neared us, I asked, "Is your bike OK, honey?"

"I'm riding in the big ring all day," he said between huffs. He had chosen to handicap himself by using his bike as if it had only one gear, a hard one.

"Why?" I asked.

"To make it more interesting," he said nonchalantly. Joe and I smiled at our boy who had set a challenge for himself and not even mentioned it.

I recall his resourcefulness even as a four-year-old. He and Katie had gone with me to meet a friend of a friend. On the way, I explained Diane didn't have children and might not understand some of the things kids need. I asked them to be as polite as they could be. After Diane and I had talked for about fifteen minutes, an eternity to pre-schoolers, Jeff asked courteously, "Do you have a garage?" He didn't want to come right out and ask if she had any tools he could play with. She showed us her garage, and she gave Jeff a hammer and a board to play with. Shortly after that, Katie asked, "Do you have a refrigerator?"

At the moment, Jeff is in the lead, and he has just stopped. Boy Scout that he is, he waits at any junction so that stragglers know which way to go. But I can't see any alternatives to the little road we're on.

"Mom," he says when I catch up to him. "Look." He points to the ground where a baby gold finch flutters at the edge of the pavement. Cheery patches of yellow feathers on its wings seem like an insult to this poor terrified baby whose wings can't yet lift her. Joe and Katie pull up next to us. I gaze above us to see two adult finches on a telephone wire. They look at the baby and step sideways back and forth on the wire, clearly agitated but not knowing what to do. Neither do I.

"I've heard that if humans touch the baby, the parents will abandon it because of our scent," I say.

Katie says, "Jeff, you definitely should not touch it."

"C'mon, little baby," I croon, "fly, fly to a bush, anywhere off the ground, not far, c'mon, you can do it." But its tiny wings aren't big enough for flight. We stand there, helpless. My memory flashes to horrific anti-fantasies that Joe and I confessed we each had when Jeff and Katie were little, images almost too awful to formulate, with our kids falling from a mountain trail in Yosemite or from our balcony loft at home.

Joe says, "All we can do is let nature take its course."

I'm having trouble abandoning this little specimen of nature, but I know we can't camp out in this spot for a week, chasing away predators. Jeff starts riding circles on his bike. Pretending I'm trying to make everybody else feel better, I say, "There don't seem to be any cars on this narrow lane, so maybe this little bird will be OK. Let's hope so."

I glance at the finches above us and swallow hard. I mentally tell them, "Sorry mom, sorry dad."

We cycle into Castrojeriz, our overnight destination, where decision-making is easy, in this case because there appears to be only one hotel to choose from. "Hotel" suggests a large enterprise, but this hotel is a small, three story building that has a sign out front, "Rooms for rent." Almost all the structures we've seen in the countryside have been stucco, either painted or naturally the same color as the surrounding dirt the stucco is undoubtedly made from. But this new-looking hotel, *La Cachava*, is sided with dark red clapboards. The wood trim is painted bright white, and an attractive black lantern graces the front door.

Joe and I read the sign in front: 33 euros for a double room.

"Can that be right?" I ask in disbelief at the cheap price.

"It's got two stars," Joe says.

"It looks a lot nicer than that."

Joe takes off his helmet and hangs it on his handlebars. The kids and I know the routine. We wait outside. Because Joe wears street clothes when he rides, he is the most normal in appearance of all of us, but even that is relative. He wears jeans shorts, very familiar at home but bizaro here. However, we figure we've got the best chance of getting a room if the hotel manager does not see four dusty, sweaty cyclists, with their bikes, rolling themselves and their dirt into the entryway.

Joe emerges with a smile on his face.

"Got 'em," he says. "The bikes go in the garage downstairs."

We stash the bikes, noticing that there is no lock on the door, which I take to be a sign of local civility. The spacious lobby looks lush and elegant with colorful carpeting and beautifully polished dark mahogany furniture. A wide, circular staircase of the same wood spirals around a knight's armor, its silver shiny and clean.

Joe's and my room has a balcony. We step onto it and behold a lovely valley of green and yellow fields. It's late in the afternoon, but the sky is still deep blue, punctuated with fluffy white clouds that look like ones I drew as a child. Actually, my artistic skills peaked in fourth grade, so I still draw clouds like this. After we shower, we invite the kids to explore town with us while we begin the big wait until dinner is served in the hotel restaurant at 9:00. Jeff and Katie decline our invitation and choose to head out on their own. We agree to meet at the hotel by 8:45, but the town is so small I won't be surprised if we bump into each other.

Joe and I stroll to the main plaza. We walk around its perimeter beneath arches supported by Moorish looking columns. It's totally quiet except for the laughter of a few children on a side street, the occasional whirr of a motorcycle, and the barking of a dog.

"This town is a funny mix of old and new," I comment. "Our hotel has recently been remodeled, but this plaza looks ancient and mostly empty. I wonder if there's a move afoot to gentrify the place? You couldn't ask for a lovelier setting."

A door swings open across the plaza. It's a little grocery store, perhaps opening after the siesta. We cross the plaza and go in. A smiling woman stands behind the counter. Shelves of wine and soft drinks line the wall behind her. Dry goods crowd the displays in the rest of the tiny space. The smells seem to have been here forever, dust and musk that have coalesced over the decades. Joe asks if she has an inexpensive bottle of wine. She quotes the price. Did I hear her right? She hands the bottle to Joe and repeats, "One euro."

A bottle of wine for about a $1.10? He selects a box of crackers, we pay, and then walk out of the plaza. We come to more new construction. It's an art gallery! How incongruous in this village. We browse. On bikes we're not likely to acquire anything to carry, but it's fun to look at the paintings, small sculptures and stained glass. I ask the woman running the gallery about the clientele, for I'm not surprised Joe and I are the only people there. She explains that she and a group of friends are hoping to build the town up, to make it a destination for Burgos tourists who'd like to visit the surrounding region. We wish her luck.

As we walk back to our hotel, I reflect to Joe, "I predict that Americans doing business in Spain would leap at the potential of this place, and they'd keep their stores open all day long, not closing for the siesta. They'd have the entire market for themselves."

"Who would want to shop then?" asks Joe. "Everybody is in siesta."

"We're not," I say. "If the Camino were in America, you can bet there would be stores and services open all day, not only here, but all along the route."

"McDonald's and 7-11 and Payday Check Cashing."

"Good point."

Back in our room, we toast.

"To Spain," says Joe. With our right elbows interlocked, we sip.

"The wine is just fine," I say.

"I agree," says Joe. "It's amazing what money can buy when the sin tax isn't factored in."

"As a lover of wine *and* language, I prefer syntax with a 'y.'"

We pull a couple of chairs onto the balcony where we sit and sip. Olive trees on the hotel lawn rustle in the light breeze, and doves I can't see keep up a steady cooing in the background. The door to Jeff and Katie's room closes, and their floorboards squeak. The kids are back. I hear the rush of pouring water and a man's muffled voice from the floor below. Maybe that's the chef, working on dinner. Whatever he's making, I know we'll enjoy every bite. I munch a few crackers and contemplate the Camino, which is snaking its way westward up out of this valley.

"I wonder if Jeff will ride that climb tomorrow morning in his big ring. Do you think he'll tackle everything in his life in ways that make it more difficult?"

"Well, we do. Riding a bike isn't the easiest way to cross this country, but we sure are enjoying it."

"You are making a lot of good points today, Joe Weed. I am reminded of why I like your company so much."

Joe steps back into the room and then returns to the balcony.

"I locked the hall door." He puts his arm around me, and just as we snuggle our way back into the bedroom together, there's a knocking on our door.

"Mom and Dad," says Jeff. "let's go see if they're

serving yet."

"We're hungry, too," I answer. Joe winks.

When we come back after dinner and re-enter our room, Joe says, "Got any room left for dessert?

"I sure do."

In the morning, we retrieve our bikes from their unlocked quarters. I say to no one in particular, "What shall we do today?"

"Let's go ridin'," says Jeff.

It takes only a few minutes to cycle out of Castrojeriz, and we pedal across the lovely valley. Then the road splits, and there's no arrow or *concha* to direct us. Joe checks our trip bible, the Camino guide.

"One way goes up and over this ridge, and the other goes through a pass. Which way do you want to go?" Joe asks in all seriousness. Katie is the first to break the silence. With the kind of sarcasm no one but a 16-year-old girl can match, she says, "Hmmm-mmmm," a diphthong with attitude. Why would she bike up a mountain if she didn't have to? To their credit, Joe and Jeff hold their testosterone in check, and we pedal toward the pass.

On this trip, the process, the journey, is the purpose. We should lengthen the part that feels good, and reduce the part that doesn't. Simple. But "feels good" is as subjective as the preference for the crust or the middle of the bread, creamy v. chunky peanut butter, or orange juice with or without pulp. So far we have compromised on what feels good for Joe and Jeff when they are in male muscle mode versus what feels good for Katie and me when we are in common sense, rational female mode.

Jeff and Katie are developing priorities as they mature. Recognizing what they like, and why, helps them create their own identities. My college students are also discovering new paradigms and patterns, fresh ways of seeing the world and themselves.

Imagine: "Let's play baseball, but we won't have any rules." How could we proceed? The rules make the game. When I assign papers to my students, I nearly always specify the length required.

"Why does it have to be that long?" students ask. Or, if it's a book review, someone might say, "There's no way I can summarize the whole book in only two pages." When Leo Tolstoy was asked to write "just a short piece," he answered, "a longer one would be easier." The challenge is deciding what to leave out. The best work contains only the essential, a boundary that word limits define.

My students are appropriately boggled by the rules of a sonnet: fourteen lines long, each with ten syllables, in iambic pentameter rhythm (that's "da-DUM" five times per line), and a highly structured rhyme scheme, too. Not only that, a sonnet is supposed to say something worth saying, and to do so poetically.

Why would anybody choose to express herself in such a tightly defined medium? Because it's art, and art's inherent boundaries pose both a creative challenge and opportunity. The canvas is the medium; paint within it. The cello is the medium; make music with it. Life is the medium; live it.

Katie cycles up next to me and says, "You look awfully serious."

"I've been thinking about the paradox that rules give us freedom."

She answers, "Yeah, right," an expression that may be the only instance in which two positives make a negative.

"Yeah, really. Like the rules that define a sonnet. The

poet uses the form to stimulate creativity."

"If those rules are so great, have you written a sonnet, Mom?"

"Good question. If I'm not going to be a hypocrite, I better write one. Tonight if I'm not too exhausted."

"How can rules give us freedom? What about curfews?" she asks.

"Curfews are catalysts reminding you to make the most of the moment. They also free you of having to say things like, 'I think you're a bore and I want to go home.' Instead, you can say, "Sorry, I need to leave now because I have a curfew."

Katie is thinking this over. If the unexamined life is not worth living, I thank the Camino for giving us an examination room.

The more I know, the more I know that I *don't* know. But I'm certain of this: Being aware of endings helps us cherish right now, because there's one curfew we all have in common.

BREAKING WIND

As we leave our hotel in Carrión de los Condes, I mentally bid farewell to the French couple I met last evening, André and Nicole. We had first seen them yesterday afternoon on the Camino. They were also cycling, but *vive la différence*. Instead of wearing a helmet, for me a safety requirement, Nicole wore a floppy pink hat tied on with a ribbon that flowed out behind her. I flashed on the terrible image of Isadora Duncan's strangling when her long scarf caught under the wheel of a car. This large woman and her smiling husband, even larger, appeared not to be worried about a thing. They waved from their vantage point on a ridge just ahead of us, and we waved back.

"I wonder how much longer those bikes will support them," said Joe. Their bikes looked like basic Sears models designed for kids to ride to school, not for hefty folks like them to ride on rough Camino trails.

When we checked into our hotel, I was delighted to see those bicycles, unsubstantial though they were, in the courtyard in front of our room. The woman emerged to hang a blouse on the clothesline. A smile is clear in any language, and we introduced ourselves to the extent she could speak English and I, French. They were cycling the entire Camino one week at a time for as many summers as it would take. I hung our kind-of washed sweaty shirts, socks and undies right next to their shorts and her bra, which looked way too delicate for such a buxom woman.

This morning, their room still looked dark, so I took our clothes off the line quietly. With a clothes pin, I tacked up a note, "*Adieu, Bon Voyage et Buen Camino.*" We will probably never see them again. In fact, most people I have ever interacted with, I will never see again. Instead of the tiresome "Have a nice day," I vote that we bid farewell to folks with whom we have had a brief exchange, "Have a nice life." In other words, *Buen Camino.*

Within a few blocks of our hotel, an alluring aroma makes our choice of breakfast stop easy. The place is more of a bakery than a café. We sit at one of the two tables crammed between the display case and the front door.

Between bites into my just-out-of-the-oven croissant, I ask, "Would anyone like to hear my sonnet?"

"Definitely," says Joe. "Will you read it to us?"

I pull out my spiral binder and flip through several pages of drafts.

"Kiddoes, remember the full name of Santiago?"

"The Moor Killer?" Jeff says.

"Yes, but no. I mean the place we're riding to."

"Santiago de Compostela, Saint James of the Starry Field," says Joe.

"I think that may be the only reference in the poem that might not be clear besides 'the merry prankster band,' which you kids probably won't recognize. That was a group of wild '60s hippies who took LSD and traveled in a bus around the country."

"This sonnet is sounding more and more interesting," says Jeff.

"OK, here goes:

My bike gives me a life behind the bars.
Its wheels go round and round but still advance
by pedal-powered, spinning legs toward stars,
the Compostela shrine far west of France.
Eight legs push up and down o'er hill and vale,
the Kendall-Weeds, a merry prankster band.
We pull and prod and laugh and coast and sail
past windmills through a luscious, grape-filled land.
The travelers flow to westward like a stream,
our vessel dusty boot or mountain bike,
all separate, yet we share the pilgrims' dream
to reach our goals that may not seem alike.
    It's not about the site we're heading for.
    The journey is life's cycle turning o'er."

"That's great, Mom!" says Katie, sounding surprised. "I especially like the line about the 'vessel' being a dusty boot or mountain bike."

"I don't think we're a merry prankster band," says Jeff. "We don't do drugs."

"We're traveling, we're merry, we are a family band, and I think pranks in good taste are allowed."

"I love this, Marty," says Joe. "Read it again so we can savor it a second time."

I take another sip of my *café con leche.*

"I guess I can find the time to do that." When I finish, I ask, "What kind of morning is it?"

"It's another beautiful morning," comes back the recitation.

We pedal out. As is typical in Spanish villages, the streets before nine in the morning are almost empty save for the omnipresent sparrows and a few shop owners sweeping or hosing down the sidewalks in front of their stores. We've been on the Camino for about a week and a half, and I am adjusting to the physical demands. Instead of being fueled purely by adrenaline, I am beginning to be fueled also by developing stamina and muscles. My cycling shorts pull on easier than they used to. Next time we pass any large windows, I'll check out my reflection to see if my legs have become rippling, sinewy, willowy power machines.

We are midway between the two largest cities of the Camino, Burgos behind us and León in front of us. We have entered the famous plains of Spain. The Camino's sun-drenched, straight hiking trail crosses flat land reminiscent of Montana's blue-domed Big Sky Country. Some fields are lush with wheat while others are lush with rocks. Joe says this seems like Ireland, only without the green.

Guiding us across fields, in the middle of nowhere, are yellow arrows painted on rocks, fence posts, and occasional tombstone-like cement pillars with *conchas* etched in them or painted on tiles. The Camino shares tractor trails, and more than once we have lifted our bikes off the trail to let a huge threshing machine drive past. The farmers smile a greeting. *Buen Camino.*

The heat grows more intense. I tell myself that the occasional breeze makes the cycling almost comfortable as we pedal the long dry miles. Farm equipment working in the fields spews up huge clouds of dust that defy science. Instead of disbursing evenly across the countryside, all the dust particles find their way to our bodies and cling to our sweaty, sunscreened arms and legs. I'm wearing my only pair of cycling shorts and my short-sleeved, used-to-be white jersey. I feel like Katie did as a four-year-old when her room was hot one summer night and she was having trouble falling asleep. I told her, "You'll be cooler if you take off your pajamas. You have too many clothes on." She thought about that and answered, "I have too much skin on."

Although most days we pass no more than a couple of dozen pilgrims, we are always aware that others have come this way before. For no apparent reason, suddenly there will be a collection of cairns alongside the trail. In this stretch, the rock piles are only a foot or two tall.

"Let's make some," I suggest on my radio.

We stop, and each of us builds a sculpture. Stone age art suits my talents perfectly.

The heat becomes exhausting. Just being alive beneath this sun demands energy. Being alive *and* riding a bike demand more energy than any sane woman in her fifties ought to consider coming up with. My mouth feels like I've been chewing on a sweater. My stomach growls for lunch. My mind longs for shade to eat it in. Surely a tree must grow somewhere on these plains. The trail passes a spot with a few pathetic dust-covered shrubs next to a dirt mound.

"This looks inviting, no?" I radio to no one in particular.

We stop. The effort of distributing the food requires my superego to assert itself over the frighteningly pushy demands of my uncomfortable id. It screams to me to find a cool swimming pool, a large shade tree, an air-conditioned Baskin-Robbins, or just an ice cold glass of water. I repress the screams, and pull my soggy shirt away from my sticky body.

We arrange ourselves on various bumps on the dirt mound. The scraggly bushes have gone limp in this oven, and they provide no shade. No one speaks as we sweat and eat, sweat and drink. I slurp my warm yogurt and slimy slices of melting cheese. I would love to have some grapes, but they are still in Joe's pannier. Standing up and walking over to get them is more work than they're worth.

After Katie finishes eating, she lies down on her back on the dirt and blocks the sun by putting her helmet over her face. I'm considering the same, but standing up again would be iffy. This heat pushes everything down. Just thinking about trying to rise from a prone position makes my eyes see stars.

"Let's go ridin'," says Jeff. "Let's find some cool mountains to climb."

The prospect of climbing mountains does not seem alluring. Nonetheless, Joe stands up, and I do too. I give Katie a hand and pull her to her feet. We stash our empty yogurt cups and wrappers back in our panniers, and we slowly pedal on, the sun holding us hostage in its hot, brilliant glare.

With the climate so dry (My Fair Lady had it wrong), how can the farmers coax anything to grow? After pedaling for who knows how many more miles, we discover one answer, an irrigation canal. A sign identifies it as the Canal de Castilla. What a relief to be near water, with trees lining the canal's banks. Water is life.

When we come across a public fountain, or as Jeff calls it, a hydration station, we stop to rest and refill our water bottles. Two men who look to be in their eighties hold dominion here, making use of the stone benches that are at least as old as they are. One gentleman wears a blue shirt, a dark red tie, and a dapper white hat. The other wears a black shirt and a black beret. In their throaty voices they respond to Joe's polite comments about the lovely setting and, as they call it, "our canal."

Joe asks where the water comes from to fill the canal. Then the trouble begins.

The man in black says, "It's from the Pisuerga River a few miles west of here, not far." He thumps the ground with his cane, a wooden exclamation point to his pearl of wisdom.

"No," says the competing sage at the fountain.

"What do you mean, 'no'?" he says.

"It's from east of here." He holds his palms up to emphasize how obvious this truth is.

"What are you saying? It's from the west. Everybody knows that," the other man says in a louder voice.

"How can you have lived here all these years and not know anything about our canal?" He is almost yelling.

"How can you have lived here all these years and not know anything about anything?" He lifts his cane and waggles it, his face a study in disbelief at the stupidity of his compadre.

"What kind of asinine fool have you become, old man?"

"What kind of ignorant idiot have you ALWAYS been, you ….!?" His body and cane shake in rage that transcends words.

We hop on our bikes and get the hell out of Dodge.

In a few kilometers, the Camino crosses the canal, the origin of its water remaining unknown. With reluctance we leave its cooling influence. We are on our way to El Burgo Raneros, the largest town in this very rural stretch. With a head wind to push against, we are plenty tired late in the afternoon when we pedal into the village, if you could even call it that.

Pilgrims converge on the low-cost dormitory, called a *refugio*. Our guidebook, as well as signs on the pilgrim refuges, make it clear that these lodgings are open only for walking pilgrims in the busy summer months. Cyclists, of which there are few, must fend for themselves. I don't mind, as a *refugio* is usually nothing more than a huge room crammed with bunk beds. The lack of privacy and amenities, not to mention the snoring of some pilgrims and the pre-dawn arising of virtually all of them, don't make a *refugio* very appealing.

We see only one alternative to the *refugio*, a two-story building across the street with a café bar on the first floor and hotel rooms advertised on the second. We lean our bikes against the building and walk inside. I'd be delighted to order something to drink, but unlike everywhere else we've been, the vibe here is not welcoming. The bar patrons glower at us. The manager says there are rooms, but they will not be available for another two hours, and we can not see them in advance of paying for them at 75 euros each, a rate suspiciously high. The prospect of waiting in this isolated and hostile place prompts Joe to say to the kids and me, "Have we got it in us to keep going?"

We agree that we do.

"Let's push on," I say.

"Push" turns out to be more than accurate. As the afternoon advances, the hot west wind slams against us with more and more power. It's a steady force that makes each rotation of the pedals result in only minor advancement for the effort I am expending. Canoeing against a tide is easier than this.

The dirt trail makes a slight bend, and we find ourselves next to a very new, very straight paved road lined with skinny saplings, all of them bent over. They are losing the battle against this Aeolian enemy. Because we see no cars, I move to the road, appreciating its smooth surface only a few feet from the rocky path. Joe, Jeff and Katie follow me. The road itself could not be any easier, and we are cycling on the level, but the wind, a four-letter word, challenges our stamina and determination.

An old farm truck approaches from behind us. We move to single file to let him pass. He is going slowly.

"Let's draft it!" Jeff yells.

"Is it safe?" I yell back.

Jeff swoops behind the truck, riding about two inches – well, maybe ten – from its rear bumper. In less than a New York minute, Joe, Katie and I join him. We ride right next to each other, handlebars occasionally touching. With the truck breaking the wind for us, our handicap is removed. We pedal at half the rate we'd been doing before, but we advance at three times the speed.

"What if he slows down? We'll slam into him!" I say, no longer needing to shout to be heard in the wind. My subtext is shrieking, "This is terrifying!"

"He won't. He knows we're here," says Jeff.

"I can't believe we're doing this!" I say.

"I think it's OK," says Joe.

Katie just keeps pedaling.

Our free ride is over too soon. The farmer turns on his signal and stretches his arm out the window. He turns left onto a side road. We resume our struggle against the wind. We all wave a thank you, which he returns. *Buen Camino.*

With darkness not far off and exhaustion long since

having overtaken us, we pedal into Mancilla de las Mulas, a town much larger than El Burgo Raneros, but so much farther along the Camino we hadn't imagined it would be our next stopping place. Because of the heat and the wind, the fifty-five miles we cycled seem like seventy-five. As in the great ride of life, the conditions, not the length, determine the nature of the experience.

Usually when we pedal into a town for the night, our arrival does not really mean we have arrived. Joe likes to pick a hotel in the historic section, and in this selection process, as in most things, he is a perfectionist. But this evening Joe does not survey all the possibilities before making a choice. We ride past a hotel, and he immediately circles back to it. The friendly matron says there is room for us at this inn. Situated above a diner, the zero-star "hotel" is incredibly cheap, only a little funky, and who cares? It is here and we are here, finally. We pay the thirty euros for the kids' room with a bathroom down the hall, and thirty-two for ours, with its own bath. We stash the bikes in the garage out back, pull our panniers from them, and wearily climb the stairs to our rooms.

After showers, the kids nap. I suggest to Joe that we let them sleep. We can scout out a restaurant and then come back and get them for dinner.

Joe and I explore the town's narrow, winding brick streets that, as is usual in the late evening, are well populated. Little boys play with soccer balls, mothers push strollers, and few cars interrupt the pedestrian flow. At first we were shocked to see toddlers playing outside at ten p.m., but now we have seen it so often, we realize this is the norm for summers in Spain.

I am not in the mood for sightseeing, much less seeking any more exercise. How about a place to eat?

That's open? And close by? We soon come across a restaurant with an outdoor, thatch-covered patio in back. I hold a table for four while Joe returns to the hotel, only a few blocks away, to get the kids.

I order dinner wine for Joe and me, and enjoy a few moments to myself. I recall that when I told friends about our upcoming ride across Spain, they asked what tour we were taking. We never take tours. We do things on our own. This we-can-handle-it attitude I learned from Joe.

My dad was many wonderful things, but he was not a do-it-yourself handyman. When we were visiting him in Florida one time, Dad mentioned that a bracket supporting an awning needed bracing. Joe volunteered to deal with it and asked Dad if he had a toolbox. Dad said, "Yes, as a matter of fact, I do. It's in the garage."

Joe's courtesy and self-control enabled him not to laugh at Dad's "toolbox," a dusty, topless shoebox containing one hammer, a pair of low-tech pliers, a couple of screwdrivers, and random nails and screws. What a contrast from Joe's packed-to-the-brim red metal toolbox whose contents and their location Joe knows better than most women know in which compartment of their purse they keep their car keys and credit cards.

Joe masters any job, whether it's a household fix or a high-tech studio challenge. It might be re-roofing our house (which we did, with him as foreman and me as grunt, the year after we met), installing a tile floor (the how-to book, knee pads, and a positive attitude were all he needed), or making an educational video (in the 1980s when we planned the project, I said, "Shouldn't we take a class in how to produce a video?" He laughed and said, "No, we can just do it." He was right.)

My memories are interrupted when Joe comes back to

the restaurant. I can't understand why he is alone. He says, "You're not going to believe this. Both kids say they would rather sleep than eat."

While ordering our dinners, we hear a clacking, whirring sound. It's coming from a stork nest we saw high on a steeple across the street. The waiter supplies the details. "That's our stork family, two parents and two babies. They bring us luck."

After the waiter has left our table, I say, "It's interesting how humans consider natural life to be 'ours.' I doubt the storks consider people to be 'theirs.'"

"Well, they bring us our babies," says Joe.

An older couple has been eyeing us from a few tables away. Joe has always said that Spanish men strike poses suitable for their being admired. This husband, a small man who looks to be in his seventies, stands and walks away from the table, about ten feet from his wife. Then he strikes a pose of high risk. He tilts his head back, holds his arm out and squeezes his boda bag. He opens his mouth, and a stream of red wine arches from the bag to his tongue. The wife is delighted that we are watching. Undoubtedly he is too, but he's pretending not to notice our noticing him. She says to us and anyone else who might be admiring her man, "He is from Asturias."

Joe says to me, "Drinking that way is traditional in that part of Spain, just west of here."

Joe and I smile and nod at her. I bet that as a bride she tossed out many a white shirt stained red during the early days of his learning-to-drink curve. Now, he's a master of the style, and they seem like a happy team.

We carry leftovers back with us in case the kids awake hungry. Blissfully, the wind has gone down with the sun, as the sailors' adage says it should. I don't normally notice how pleasant the absence of wind can be – especially not having to break wind – but on this still night I take Joe's hand and say, "It's another beautiful evening."

DOING IT

An hour west of Mancilla de las Mulas, I'm caught up in the polyrhythm of my rotating legs and the random clatter of my bouncing handle bar bag as my hairbrush, camera, passport, credential, chapstick, kleenex and wallet continually rearrange themselves inside it. The only constant is the grinding undercurrent of my tires gripping hard-packed dirt as we cross this endless flatland of fields and more fields.

We're cycling a tractor trail. On the right track, I turn up the revs and catch up to Jeff, who's in the lead on the left.

"Hey, honey, would this be a good course for a long cross-country race?"

"No."

"Because?"

"It's flat and boring."

"How could we make this more interesting?" I ask.

"It's fine, Mom. I'm not complaining," he says. He wheelies, and even though he's riding on only one tire, he easily pulls ahead of me.

"*You* are making life more interesting," I call out to him. As I watch his muscled arms lift his handlebars up, I flash to the memory of baby Jeffy Joe in his cushioned blue infant seat placed on top of the kitchen counter, his little arms outstretched when he was ready to be picked up. I tear up and hum one of the jazz standards I often sing at gigs, "I'm a Sentimental Sap, That's All."

Here in the plains, there's no mist other than in my eyes. Jeff resumes two-wheeling, and I wonder how Katie and Joe are doing behind me. I risk my balance by making a quick turn of the head backwards to see. Katie is pedaling steadily, the picture of fashion in her black cycling shorts and stretchy black tank top. Joe rides behind her. We're rollin'.

Yesterday's challenge against the wind raised the ante, and we made it. We are doing well. Yes, doing. That's the key. As a former child, I remember the mantra, "Mother, I'd rather do it myself." In my teaching life, I am passionate about helping my students become successful doers. In traditional classrooms, while the teacher is speaking, thinking, pacing, writing on the board, gesturing, and evidencing other signs of engagement with the subject, too many students look like dead people sitting up.

The solution? Let the students do the work.

I imagine a member of my college's Board of Trustees (I'll call him B.T.) saying to faculty at a packed Board meeting, "Students are blank slates and it's your job to fill them up."

I answer on behalf of the faculty. "If students are blank slates when it comes to understanding literature, then listening or pretending to listen to a lecture about it won't teach them how to understand, much less appreciate literature when there's no lecturer around. Students need to become their own lecturers, their own teachers."

B.T. retorts, "If students can teach themselves, then why do we need teachers?"

A million, or at least five, answers jump to mind.

Diane Ackerman says that "life is indeed the best teacher, but the tuition is high." Instead of casting each individual out to sea to learn to navigate on his or her own, civilization expedites the learning process, passing along wisdom, survival strategies, and conveniences like running water and microwaves. Some people might love inventing wheels, but others might prefer to invent bicycles, or just to ride them. Education gives people a foundation of knowledge from which they can select a particular field that piques their curiosity or inspires their creativity.

I say, "B.T., you're right. I can't teach a student anything."

There's a gasp in the Board Room, the Vice Chancellor of Instruction nervously reaches for a drink of water, the President of the Faculty Union looks up from his notes, and the press corps shows signs of awakening.

I say, "Nobody can teach a student anything. The role of teachers is to serve as catalysts who create situations that inspire and facilitate students' learning."

"For example?" asks B.T., working hard to look open minded as the photographer aims his camera at him.

"In my required Intro to Literature course last year, I assigned Sophocles' *Oedipus Rex*. To help students learn the process of interpretation, I wrote open-ended questions that I cut out and put in a wicker basket. My work was done. Then it was the students' turn to learn by doing. When class began, I announced that we would be having a party, and I drew a martini glass on the board."

At the mention of a martini, I have the full attention of the entire Board of Trustees.

"Then I drew the prohibited sign across the glass to show that there would be no alcohol. I told my students, 'For our party, I'd like each of you to choose a slip of paper from the basket. Every slip contains a different question about *Oedipus Rex*. When I say, 'Let the party begin,' I want you all to stand up and mingle, discussing with as many classmates as you can the questions you picked. In about twenty minutes, the mingling will be over, and I'll ask each of you to read your question aloud and then give your opinion after you have considered the input of your classmates.' I played the host serving sparkling cider and crackers as I circulated around the room."

B.T. says with not too much sarcasm, "Standing around talking – that's education?"

"In this case, absolutely. All thirty students were actively discussing the literature. The party time couldn't be shined on as a gabfest, because at the end, everyone in class expected everyone else to say something worth listening to. Students discovered that by talking about the issues, they themselves could piece together many possible ways of understanding the play."

The ring-ring of my radio interrupts my Board Room scenario. Katie is calling to Jeff who, as usual, leads the way.

She says, "Jeff, see any urination stations up there?"

"Yeah, there are some bushes looking pretty dry," he answers. "I'll wait for you."

Why are most of the teenage boys I know amused by anything that has to do with noisy, smelly body effusions? Brushing teeth isn't fun or funny. Combing hair isn't fun or funny. But a loud belch or fart? Absolutely hilarious. After we catch up to Jeff, I ignore his crude imitations of unpleasant body noises as Katie tries to disappear discreetly behind the shrubbery. What a relief to *have* some shrubbery after yesterday's open, arid, no-place-to-hide landscape.

After we get back on our bikes, my mental wheels resume. I reflect on the Tom Sawyer corollary to the value of doing it. Make painting the fence such a desirable activity that people will pay for the chance to do it. If someone told me, "You have to cross Spain on a bicycle," my American notion of freedom would be offended. "I don't have to do anything I don't want to, so there." We had to *want* to ride our bikes across Spain.

I want students to see that the units gained in my courses are worth the time they are spending and the tuition they are paying, and to realize that they are not just inching their way toward a degree, but also gaining insight about why humans act as we do. Students are not going to come to a grand liberal arts enlightenment by listening, or pretending to listen, to a lecture. As Plutarch said, "The mind is not a vessel to be filled, but a fire to be ignited."

Why do I chuckle when Katie cycles up next to me and says with her perfect sarcasm, "Oh good, another hill." Why do we pedal up it without much complaint? Because we know we chose to make this trip, and we will feel proud of ourselves at the hilltop. We will have done it. When students discover that literature provides an opportunity to explore truths about themselves, they'll get in line for the chance to climb the hill.

At the top of this particular hill, we have a vista that shows the historic city of León in the distance. As we approach it, the number of roads, cars, buildings and people steadily increases, a bustling contrast to the peace and solitude we've grown accustomed to while crossing the rural plains. We behold a modern freeway. Vehicles barrel along in their race to somewhere. The smell of exhaust seems particularly obnoxious probably because we've been in an almost car-free environment for days. A tall, new looking bridge crosses over the freeway, and that's where the Camino leads us.

I huff and puff my way up the steep ramp and pedal across the bridge. The ramp down, I note casually, is coated with gravel.

I begin the descent to the level where the Camino turns a sharp right. The gravel on the ramp is much deeper than I suspected. My wheels sink into it. Not good. The more I try to slow down, the more I find myself skidding. I brake gently, reminding myself to squeeze and let go, squeeze and let go, but nothing changes.

Yikes!

By the time I slide to the bottom of the ramp and onto the trail, my completely-out-of-control bike, on which I happen to be a passenger, has drifted way too far to the left. The trail is coated with gravel that has spilled from the ramp, so I still can't get traction or control. My left-veering arc continues, inch-by-inch closer to the trail's edge, defined by a waist-deep ditch.

I've heard people describe an accident saying, "It happened so fast." I am not saying that. This is happening slowly. Agonizingly slowly. I know what I'd do on a horse, so I try it. I lean right, I pull the handlebars to the right, and I look right, but the gravel understands physics better than I do. I find myself moving left, left, left, ever closer to the three-foot-deep ditch. Then, science wins.

Shit! Shit! Shit! Shit! In the nanosecond my brain allows me to plan for what seems imminent disaster, I swear I will *not* get hurt, I will *not* go over the bars. I will stay vertical, whether the bike is under me, over me, or next to me.

My front wheel dives from the trail. I fling my right arm out to grab the ground, and with my left I push the bike away from me. My feet, running and stumbling, land on the bottom of the ditch. I don't know what has happened to my bike.

"Mom's down!" Joe yells into his radio for the kids to hear.

Before I can get my wits about me and figure out how I am, much less how I might get out of the ditch, my family reaches me, the kids having heard Joe's message. Jeff and Joe lean over, each grabbing one of my hands. They pull me back up to the trail.

"Are you OK?" Joe asks repeatedly. Jeff retrieves my bike.

My heart and head are racing. It is hard to calm down enough to assess my condition, but I recognize that I am not badly hurt, but totally shaken. My right shoulder is throbbing, and I have a red badge of courage in the form of a scraped, bloodied right arm. But these physical messages to my brain seem minor compared to my shrieking emotions.

I am freaking out not from what happened, but from what didn't.

Thanks to nothing but good luck, my cycling incompetence has not caused me to be seriously injured, a catastrophe that would make us abort the whole adventure. I have come way too close to ruining this for everybody.

I look at Joe, attempt a smile, and take a deep breath.

"I'm OK."

"I'm glad, Mommy," Katie says, her voice sounding more worried than relieved. Another breath.

"I need a minute …."

Another breath.

Joe reaches to put his arm around me, but I pull away. My shoulder and arm are still too tender to be touched.

I've twirled into the twilight zone of shock.

Everybody is staring at me and responding to my fear. I've got to pull myself together.

Another breath.

Jeff slowly pours water from his Camelbak over my wound.

"I'm cleaning your road rash off, Mom," he says. In charge of carrying the first aid kit, he pulls out the bandages and hands them one by one to Joe. After the water dries, Joe gently puts them on my arm to help stop the bleeding.

I've got to break out of my personal panic. Say something, voice.

"I'm really OK."

I watch Joe's careful doctoring of my arm. I am taken care of. All will be well. We are so incredibly, wonderfully, marvelously lucky.

As Joe applies the last of the bandages, I ask Jeff, "How did you manage not to skid out of control on the ramp?"

"I know how to ride a bike," he says.

Joe says, "You can't brake your front wheel on a downhill without skidding."

"Which brake controls the front wheel?"

"The left one, Mom," Jeff says. "That's so beginners won't panic and hit the front brake with their right hand, usually the stronger one, and end up catapulting themselves over the bars."

"How can I have ridden three hundred miles and never noticed which brake lever controls which brake?" I ask.

No one answers. It is an awkward silence. To her credit, Katie does not say, "Hmm-mmm."

"Life is humbling," I say.

Joe finishes taping the bandage on.

"When I fell off a horse, I always got back on, at least when I was physically able to. I'm ready for some more time behind the bars, but first, how about a Team Kendall-Weed hug? Just don't squeeze hard."

There's a lot to love in León. After the quiet countryside we've just crossed, this thriving city is energizing, and I'm ready to focus on positive energy. Pedestrians crowd the narrow streets downtown. We get off our bikes and walk in the throng. As we enter the old part of the city, a mime on our right smiles from her pedestal. On her head is a mass of flowers, a living crown that completely hides her hair. Her face is white, and her lips are painted into a delicate, permanent smile. Her filmy white dress and billowing sleeves sway in the breeze. She stands motionless, holding a wand. A little boy puts a coin in the box at her feet, and she bows, waves her wand, and blows him a kiss. Embarrassed, he scoots off. She resumes her still position, a lily shimmering above the sea of humanity.

We continue into the center of the old city. I can imagines centuries' worth of walkers, riders and carriages on these ancient streets. We stop in at a couple of hotels, but of course don't choose one quickly. Then we spy the hotel meant for us, Guzmán El Bueno. A friendly clerk in our post office at home is Art Guzmán. We get two rooms here for forty-two euros each. The hotel manager gives us a postcard with a picture of the hotel, and we address it to Art. I predict he'll have it tacked up at his station by the time we get back.

"I might buy a souvenir here," says Katie.

"Get one of those giant bulls," says Jeff. "It'd look great in our yard."

He's referring to the larger-than-life black bull silhouettes that appear on random vantage points across the country. The oversized symbol used to be a logo for Spanish Osborne brandy, but now it seems to be a mark of Spanish pride.

"We could have bull riding contests in our driveway," says Katie.

"Who will clean up the bullshit?" I ask

"Can you believe what Mom just said?" says Katie in mock horror. "Mom, I didn't hear that. Would you say that again?"

"No way, José. And here's José now."

Joe emerges from the bathroom, with his hair wet and his almost clean white shirt on.

"We're eager to be sight seers," I tell him.

"León. Lay it *on* me!" he says.

We explore the main plaza, dominated by the landmark gothic cathedral. It is light beige, apparently having recently been cleaned, and it's stunning in the late afternoon sunshine. In the plaza in front of it, a bench is occupied by a statue of a pilgrim holding a walking stick. I sit next to him, put my hand on his knee, and Jeff snaps my picture.

We walk through bustling streets and come across a crowd focused on something on the ground in front of them. We go close to investigate. It's a one-man marionette show.

"How odd we humans are," I comment to Katie. "All this activity is going on, and what do people choose to look at? Some tiny pretend characters, dangling on strings from a man's hands."

"Maybe make-believe is more interesting than reality?"

We walk further. "Look," I say to Katie and point across the street. A bride in a long white gown is sitting in the middle of the steps of a church. Her skirt is spread across the stairs. Three steps above her, standing, is the groom, posing with a haughty air as he leans nonchalantly with one hand against the church wall. A photographer is hard a work, his camera mounted on a tripod on the sidewalk

"Those steps must be filthy. I doubt it was her idea to sit there. Whose idea do you suppose it was?"

"Hmmm-mmm," says Katie.

I wonder how much of that pose is staged and how much reflects that couple's reality. I think back to Joe's and my wedding. We got married in our yard with a view of the Pacific Ocean as the backdrop. Having played music at dozens of weddings, we had no interest in a conventional ceremony. Joe's brother flipped a coin to determine who would begin the vows. Joe was first to say, "I do." When my turn came, I said, "I sure do." And we still do.

At dinner, Joe asks, "Want to spend two nights here, like we did in Burgos? Marty, is your arm sore?"

Katie says, "If your arm is bothering you, Mom, I'm happy to hang out here."

Jeff says, "Ditto."

"Thanks, everybody. If I sleep on my left side, my shoulder should be fine. I'll just keep a bandage on my arm. How long is the next stretch, Joe?"

"The book says it's sixty kilometers to Astorga, about forty miles, so it's not too far, not too close. We'll be leaving the plains, so it should get cooler as we go farther west and come to the mountains."

"I could actually move along. Now that I know which lever controls the front brake, I'm ready to ride," I say.

"Me, too," says Katie. "But I want to browse in some of the shops for a souvenir before we leave."

I meet Joe's eyes and smile. I wonder if his thoughts match mine. We were worried that Katie would not buy into this trip, and now she's eager to buy a souvenir to remember it. I'll help her pick out anything, no matter how large.

She does choose an Osborne bull. It's black, and it's on a bright red t-shirt.

THE JOY OF WRITING

"Don't brake so much, Mom. Don't fight gravity. Let it help you," says Jeff. After delivering this advice, he turns and drops off the edge of the earth. The steep, rutted and very rocky trail careens down a cliff west of León. Jeff rips down it, child's play for him. Joe goes next, flexing his knees, with an air of being comfortably in charge.

I graciously say to Katie, "After you, my sweet." She stands up on her pedals and cruises down. She makes it look not exactly easy, but manageable. Go, girl! As for me, it's moments like this when I wish we'd had more children.

My mind transplants me to Squaw Valley on the summit of Siberia, a ski slope as user friendly as the name suggests. On a ledge at its top, most skiers find a reason to pause. They tighten their boots, adjust their goggles, or take a swig of their beverage of choice. Once you push off that ledge, there's a straight down "this is it" moment of truth until you gather your composure to turn against the vertical careening and gain some control over your fate.

But I love Siberia. It demands my best skiing skills, gets my pulse rate going, and at the bottom of the slope, I'm exhilarated.

I adjust my helmet.

I retie my shoes.

I take a swig of water.

I would be lying if I were to say that I attacked this rocky downhill with total abandon, never using my brakes and flying from ridge to valley in one graceful arc. But I make a mantra of Jeff's advice, "Don't brake, don't brake," quashing my inclination to think of it as, "Don't break, don't break." Thanks to my work-in-progress panic control, I make myself use the brakes less often than my survival instinct urges me to. When I get to the bottom, still feeling winded from the anxiety (note to self: breathe next time), Jeff says, "You're starting to get the idea, Mom."

"Thanks, honey. I appreciate your encouragement. That's even nicer than your compliment after my Woz book came out. Do you remember what you said?"

"No."

"It's the first book you've written that isn't boring."

"I'm sure I meant it," says Jeff with a smile.

Now that we're back cycling on semi-level ground, I indulge in the memory of my 9-year-old Jeffy Joe. He was in fourth grade, and he'd just read the first edition of *Steve Wozniak, Inventor of the Apple Computer.* I was pleased by his high praise, but I didn't offer up that quote to the newspaper. I was hoping that professional reviewers might be just a tiny bit more positive. *Booklist* delivered, saying the book was "sure to fascinate readers."

The first key in publishing, however, is not fascinating readers or reviewers. The person to fascinate is the editorial director at the publishing house who determines whether or not there will even be a book. If our Camino trip can be called a bikathon, then I guess I can say I've already done a submitathon. After writing four biographies for young readers, I felt ready to try something new. I wrote a story called *Piñata Party.* Because the publishers I'd worked with focused on the school library market, and this picture book was suited for the trade market, I searched for a new publisher. I bought the annual *Writer's Market* and began submitting my manuscript, which is the text. I do windows, but I don't do illustrations. I sent it to all the publishers of children's picture books that began with A. They all responded "No thanks." So I sent it to publishers starting with B. They all responded, "No thanks." I did the same for the publishers starting with C. Same results. By the time I got rejections from all the publishers starting with D, I was starting to feel Discouraged.

I asked myself, "Should I move on to something else and get a life, or continue subjecting myself to form letter after form letter that essentially says I am a terrible writer, the book was a ridiculous idea, and just who do I think I am?"

I kept submitting.

Piñata Party did find a publisher – Willowisp. This true story demonstrates the masochism required to be a published author.

We cycle into a little town, really barely a hamlet, but it's got a public fountain. Jeff has stopped by it, and the rest of us follow suit.

"This is such a great tradition," I say as I pull my water bottle from the pannier.

"Drinking water?" says Jeff.

"The availability of fresh water in every town," I say, leaning over to refill my bottle from the spigot.

"I bet for a lot of rural villages, the public fountain used to be the only water source," says Joe. "Spain has only recently arrived in the 20th Century. When I was here thirty years ago, the countryside was still primitive."

"The European Union has given Spain a huge boost.

It looks like somebody went overboard in road building, though. We have ridden a lot of roads that cars don't seem to use," I say.

"That's OK with me," says Katie. "Smooth is good."

Joe takes his turn to refill his water bottles.

"We're definitely out of the plains and into the hills, but where's the cool air?" I ask.

"Let's go find it," says Jeff, and he pushes off.

Once we've returned to the road, my mind returns to my writing, and the need of people like me to produce words and more words. Maybe it's the same as Joe's compulsion to produce music.

It seems to me that some people generally prefer to be observers who receive input, while others prefer to generate output. When students in my required composition class say, "I don't know what to write about," I suspect they are in the first group. To help students like this, Robert Pirsig advises that they look at familiar things more closely, to see them in a fresh way. I love his assigning students at the University of Montana to observe their thumb nail and then write about it. Because they'd never read anything about a thumb nail, he knew they would have to look at it for themselves, seeing something original and more interesting than clichés. Samuel Johnson said a good writer should make a new subject familiar and a familiar subject new. Anne Lamott suggests beginning writers seek detail in their own past, starting with their elementary school lunches. In my case, that's a bunch of baloney. Sliced thin.

Writing by choice can be both indulgence and obsession. For me, it's an extension of my teacherly soul. I don't regret my decision to turn down a publisher's offer to write biographies of Civil War generals. Their lives may have been interesting, but I don't want to study men who led armies. For kids, I choose subjects that I find personally inspiring, or at least fun.

I remember the moment I decided to write a song for kids. It was a school morning when Jeff was seven, and Katie six. Both of them arrived at the breakfast table wearing jeans with holes in the knees. (Point of truth: They still do.)

I said, "After breakfast, why don't you put on some nicer jeans. You can leave the ones you're wearing on your beds, so they'll be handy to put on when you get home."

"But Mom, I can't pay attention in school if I'm not comfortable," said Katie. Talking to her has always been like talking to a miniature adult.

Jeff piped up, "What's wrong with these? I like 'em."

"They just don't look very nice for school. I used to have school clothes and play clothes."

Katie said, "These jeans are my favorites."

"Do we *have* to change?" said Jeff, every syllable exuding frustration.

I thought for a moment, reflected on the kids' good grades and their abundance of friends. "No, you don't. You can learn just as much at school whether your jeans are holey or not."

I decided to write a song that celebrates jeans. I wrote lyrics to *Redwing*, a fiddle tune whose melody I was surprised to see in Katie's Suzuki violin book. There it was called *The Happy Farmer*, excerpted from Schumann. Now, I sing *My Old Jeans* to myself in rhythm with my pedaling.

My jeans, my jeans,
My old and faded jeans.
They're big and baggy, soft and saggy,

My old jeans.
My mother says, "They're way too ragged now,"
But I don't care, I love to wear them anyhow.

They're my old jeans, my favorite old jeans.
I think they love me, they always hug me.
They're my old jeans, my favorite old jeans.
They are my close friends for work and play.

My jeans, my jeans,
They let the breezes blow.
The knees are holey, guacamole!
Where did they go?
They fit just right, they never feel too tight.
They're comfy, cozy, warm and rosy, my old jeans.

They're my old jeans, my favorite old jeans.
I think they love me, they always hug me.
They're my old jeans, my favorite old jeans.
They are my close friends for work and play.
They are my close friends for every day.

Heat takes my attention away from my humming. The Camino continues to climb, and now we're on a dirt trail. It is a narrow catchall for cobbles, a textbook example of what happens when there's no erosion control. Scraggly scrub oaks line the edge, but they are too short to provide shade. Often I have to get off and push my bike because I can't get traction at my slow pace to pedal uphill over the loose rocks.

As the sun intensifies, so does my thirst. The smell of dust adds to the dryness. Joe calls out, "Rest stop." Bathed in sweat, he sits down under the only tree large enough to fit under. Like Joe, the rest of us carry panniers, but unlike him, we do not also carry a backpack and a big professional video camera slung around our neck. He also carries more than one very large water bottle. At this moment in the afternoon, he is clearly the most winded of the four of us.

"Let's have a hydration celebration," says Jeff.

We all drink from our water bottles, not caring that the sun has warmed the water.

"Need help carrying anything, Dad?" Jeff asks. "I've got room on my bike."

"No, thanks," says Joe.

"Because of all the gear you are carrying, this is way harder than your morning rides," I say to Joe. "One time at the store I was chatting with Eric as he rang up the groceries. I heard a guy behind me in line talking about a saint he drives past every morning riding his bike up Mt. Bache Road. I turned and said, 'That's my husband, but I'm not sure he's a saint.' The man said, "I didn't say 'he's a saint.' I said, 'He's insane.'"

To lengthen the rest time, I offer to shoot some video. My sane saint hands me the camera, and I say, "Jeff and Katie, will you please perform for your fans?"

They demonstrate their evolving handshake routine. It includes parallel moves in the air, an occasional tapping of knuckles, a cameo appearance of thumbsies, and a moment of exaggerated, old-fashioned handshaking.

Finally Joe stands up. Seeing no need to rush his recovery, I say, "Let's slather up with another dose of sunscreen. Look at our left arms and legs. Moss may grow on the north side of a tree, but skin gets tan on the south side of the limbs."

"Profound, Mom," says Katie.

"I second that lotion," says Jeff as he reaches for the

sunscreen.

"Myrtle laugh," I say.

He squeezes a dollop of sunscreen into everybody's palms, and we rub ourselves down.

I wonder if this climb will lead us to cooler mountain air, and if so, when. Joe still looks beat, so I suggest we all take one more drink.

"A toast," I say, "to Sam Williams, whose generosity helped make this trip possible."

Everyone obliges and pulls out water bottles again. We get back on our bikes, and I think about Sam, a student during my first years at City College. He grew up dirt poor in rural Michigan where his father worked on the railroad, and his mother was a maid.

Sam served in Vietnam and then moved to the Golden State of opportunity. Thanks to the G.I. Bill, he enrolled at City College and took one of my composition classes. He had weak writing skills, but he was a doer. He founded the Black Student Union and asked me to be the faculty advisor. With some reservations about whether his peers would accept a person of Caucasian persuasion, I agreed.

When Sam introduced me as the club advisor, nobody in the handful of the club's first members spoke out against his choice. I relaxed, and we had fun. We planned a fundraiser, recruited new members, and at their urging, I performed with musician friends on the quad to draw attention to new student organizations getting started in the mid-1970s. (At our commuter college of mostly part-time, low-income students, social activism lagged way behind that of the more affluent Berkeley to the north). In those days, I was regularly taken to be a student, for I looked the part and practically played it, too. I parted my wavy brown hair in the middle, wore hip hugger, bellbottom jeans, a puka shell necklace, and madras cotton blouses over my braless bosom.

It wasn't until years later that I learned that while Sam was engaged in student activities on campus, he was usually broke. He sometimes slept in his car, parked on a side street near the college. He never complained to me about his situation, so I had no idea what his personal life was like.

Sam graduated and transferred to San Jose State. For him and most students, there is life after City College. I have yet to experience it myself.

Years passed, and my memory of Sam faded. Then in 1999, I received a phone call from a man who introduced himself as "Sam Williams' accountant."

"Sam Williams' accountant?"

"Sam has formed a charitable foundation, and he would like you to be a board member." He told me where and when the first meeting would be. I accepted the invitation although I had no idea what a board member of a charitable foundation was supposed to do. The afternoon before the first meeting, I felt downright nervous. What would be expected of me? What was I getting into? I also felt like I did not *look* the part, whatever the part was. My day in/day out leather blazer was faded, and its cuffs were fraying. "I'm shabby-looking!" I thought. "I can let the kids wear holey jeans to school, but as for me, I need some retail renovation."

I decided I would get a nice looking, practical, multi-purpose coat, one a Board Member would not be ashamed to wear to a Board Meeting. I meandered around the women's section at Sears. As usual when I'm confronted with merchandise overload, nothing appealed to me. Then, a rack of black raincoats caught my eye and then my hand; their soft, suede-like texture felt good. I tried one on. Too long. I tried another. Still too long. Then I tried a Small Petite. YES! I looked at the tag. This was a lined London Fog, not an imitation, and the sale(!) price was $250. I had never seriously considered buying any article of clothing for anywhere near that amount of money.

I bought it, put it on, and drove to the meeting on the third floor of a downtown bank building.

As I got off the elevator, my palms rubbing against the comforting soft fabric of the coat, I worried that I might not even recognize Sam. I hadn't seen him in more than twenty years. I walked into the meeting room and was immediately greeted by Sam.

"Ms. Kendall," he said, "you've let your hair grow."

I laughed out loud. What a gentleman! Besides having longer hair, I had gained more than a few wrinkles, yet Sam found something nice to say.

"Sam, how great to see you!" I said. He looked the same and more – about sixty pounds more.

At our third or fourth Board meeting, Sam asked, "What stipend do you think the Board Members should get?"

The fact that money for us had not been mentioned had made me assume that my position was simply an honor, and I would donate my time and efforts to the charity. One Board member said, "How about $20,000 a year?" Was he kidding?

Sam said, "That would be fine."

I looked at the other Board member, who smiled and said, "I second that." I couldn't stop myself. I jumped up, reached across the table and shook Sam's hand. "Thank you, I can't believe this, this is amazing, it's a HUGE amount for me!"

"You're welcome," said Sam, embarrassed, trying to sit back down, obviously wishing I knew some protocol. He, the hick from Michigan, was accustomed to dealing with large sums of money. I, a hick in the world of high finance, was accustomed to dealing with large stacks of papers to grade.

Over the course of a few years, we fulfilled Sam's vision to give the Foundation's money away in scholarships to students at City College, two other local community colleges, and San Jose State. When its funds were depleted, the Foundation was dissolved. But it's because of those stipends that I am able to make this trip without taking out a loan. Thank you, Sam, for remembering me, for sharing your wealth with a teacher you had years ago, and for setting up a foundation that helped students not have to sleep in their cars as you did.

Remembering Sam has helped me forget my worries about Joe's being overloaded with heavy gear. We are pedaling slowly up a long, hot ascent. We make it to the top of the hill, and ah-ha, there is a lovely view, with the town of Astorga, our destination, on the opposite side of the small, neatly farmed valley in front of us. We are almost there. We coast down the hill. I am cooled by my evaporating sweat and comforted by how close we are to today's destination.

We ride into town and immediately spy on our right the striking palace designed by Gaudi, Spain's most famous architect. Its odd angles, tall graceful curves and gray stonework shout "Gaudi" from the turret tops. Even more delightful to me are the residents of the turret tops, black and white storks who nest in all the best places, the highest a city can offer. Storks are big, and their nests are even bigger. Gaudi's creation is topped by nature's creation, the creatures that we credit with delivering our own creations to us.

Our hotel is the nicest one we've indulged in so far. In fact, it's the first place we've spent the night that actually feels like a hotel. It's the new, three-star Astur Plaza at almost twice the price of the hotel in Nájera, the only other three-star one we've stayed in. It's still reasonable by American standards, though, at 65 euros per room.

The bathroom demonstrates once again that Europeans like to get their feet wet. That's why they don't enclose showers. Actually, this modern bathroom has a glass shower door that goes almost half way across the opening. I'd have loved to overhear the conversation in which that decision was made:

"Let's put in a shower door."

"Why?"

"When there's water on the floor, people can slip. They could sue us."

"This is not America, don't worry."

"What if Americans stay here?"

"They never do."

"They might pay well."

"We'd have to charge enough to cover their law suits, and then nobody else could afford to stay here."

"Let's compromise with a half door."

We see no other Americans, and for the record, we are not planning to slip or to sue. Unlike the other bathrooms in hotels we've stayed in so far, this one also has a counter next to the sink so we don't need to keep our toiletries in the lake on the floor. For the very first time on this trip, we're staying in a hotel that has an elevator. We don't need to climb one or two or three flights of stairs carrying our panniers and handlebar bags, and sometimes our bikes, too. These are high living, deluxe accommodations. Life is good on the pilgrim trail.

Now I'm sitting at one of the many small, inviting round tables in front of the hotel, sipping a glass of crisp white wine. In front of me, the large plaza is filled with the noisy spectrum of Spanish society enjoying this pleasant evening. Parents hold the hands of the youngest children, but older boys are free to yell as they pass soccer balls back and forth. Three little girls squeal with delight as they play jump rope, trading off who swings and who jumps. Filling the benches, old folks assess the state of the world and themselves. Couples sit at the many open-air tables, and waiters bring them snacks and drinks. Above, black swifts screech, swoop and soar around the buildings that surround the plaza.

To my right stands the dominant structure, a tall, ornate government edifice. It appears to be very old and well maintained, with bright red, yellow and green filigree decorating its huge clock. Like a benevolent dictator, the clock surveys the whole plaza. Beneath the clock are two life-sized, automated knights, each holding a large metal hammer. They spring to life, taking turns swinging at a giant bell. It rings eight times. The locals take no heed, but I am mesmerized by the grandeur of the chimes and the playfulness of the mechanical men hammering time along.

Seated to my left is a guy with movie-star-handsome good looks. He's slim and tan. He wears a white dress shirt, dark blue levi's, and aviator sunglasses. He's also sipping a glass of wine. He turns toward me, and I smile.

He says, "When you and the kids are ready, do you want to go to dinner?"

"I sure do."

WHAT GOES 'ROUND

This stretch of the Camino is cut into the side of a tree-covered hill. Reducing the dust are the leaves, cones, seeds, twigs and other organic residue that carpet the trail. What I appreciate most is the blessed shade.

Without warning, my bike almost stops even though I'm still pedaling. At least I'm going slowly enough that it's not that all-too-familiar situation of cantering toward a jump, having my horse stop right in front of it and me continuing into or over it. The problem here is not an uncooperative horse. It's a flat front tire.

"Jeff," I call on my radio, "are you still my favorite mechanic?"

He turns around, not on his green Bontrager bicycle, but on a shining white steed. I step aside and hand him my limping pony.

I lean against the hillside, sip my water, and watch Jeff assess the situation.

"I think there's probably a thorn in your tire, Mom," he says. He opens his panniers, takes out tools, and begins to work.

"Can you talk while you do that?" I ask him.

"I could sleep while I do this."

"Did you enjoy teaching the Boy Scouts how to change a tire?"

"Yeah, I guess."

"I heard from the parents that you did a great job," I say. "I think you're a natural at teaching. The younger kids in the troop look up to you. And it's obvious you liked being a counselor at camp."

"Parts of it were fun," he says.

"I could picture you being a high school math teacher who coaches the cycling team on the side."

"High schools don't have cycling teams."

"You could start one."

Katie joins in. "At school Jeff already has a team of fans. When Jeff rides his BMX bike down the handrails by the back steps, a crowd of kids stands around watching him. They all have bikes, but they just hold them, drooling."

I'm slowed down by the image of drooling teenagers, but I regain my focus on the direction I want this conversation to go in.

"Do you teach them how to do your tricks?" I ask.

"It's something you learn by doing. You can't really explain it to anybody."

"I agree about the importance of learning by doing, but I bet those kids are also learning from your example."

"I don't know. I just ride."

I watch him work methodically, pulling the tube from the tire, and then scrutinizing it, inch by inch, searching for the cause of the flat.

"It's a thorn, Mom," he says.

"Will you patch the tube, or replace it?"

"I'll replace it."

"Do you think you're good at BMX just naturally, or is it because of how much you do it, or both?"

"I don't know."

"I think inborn talent is fundamental for big success in almost anything. I've heard performers play all the right notes on a violin, but they still don't make music. They may have technical chops, but they lack soul. The simplest melody, played with feeling, moves me far more than a difficult but meticulously delivered solo that sounds memorized, mechanized and metronomed."

Jeff fits the tire back into the rim.

"When it comes to teaching, the most effective instructors I've known are passionate about their subject and about helping other people develop a passion for it too. A good teacher can become better with practice and a willingness to try new things, but without that fundamental teaching instinct, I don't think someone is likely to inspire many learners. Jeff, I think you could be a great teacher, if that's what you choose to do."

"Yeah, I might like that," he says.

"Teachers are optimists, believing that they can make a difference in their students' lives. When I updated Steve Wozniak's biography, he told me he had two ambitions as a child: to design a computer and to become a teacher. He fulfilled them in that order."

"Didn't he teach in his garage?" says Jeff.

"Yes. Long after Apple's success, he pulled the Hummers out of his garage to make a custom classroom where he could teach kids, as he put it, 'to love computers on the inside and out.' Steve told me his joy in teaching came from seeing the kids' happiness when they learned something new."

Jeff has started pumping the tire up, so I take a final sip of water, and get ready to remount my pony.

We leave this hillside behind only to spy more ridges ahead of us. The wind has been picking up. As we climb, I delight in the cooler air and the energy I always get from mountains. The work of climbing is canceled out by the exhilaration of this fresh breeze.

"Anybody else getting ready for lunch?" I radio to the Team.

"Sure," answers Jeff first.

He pulls up next to random boulders not far from the trail, and we all join him. We take picnic supplies from our panniers and arrange ourselves on the rocks. We've learned to sit within passing distance of each other so we can share cheese, mortadella and chocolate without having to get up.

Under the brilliant sky, the dark green shrubs almost glow, and yellow wildflowers and gray-green lichen peak out between cracks in the boulders.

"Notice the slate rock?" I say. "Slate, in case you were dying to know, is metamorphosed shale. Here's a vocab opportunity: What's 'meta'?"

"It's a verb, as in 'I never met a word I didn't like,'" says Katie, not quite succeeding in keeping a straight face.

"And everybody knows that 'morph' means 'form,' right? So, metamorphic rock changed form, usually as a result of heat and pressure over a long time. I imagine that the shale originally here got metamorphosed when these mountains formed. That's your geology lesson for today."

"Hey, Katie," says Jeff. "Would this make a good place to take our Christmas card picture?"

I am totally surprised. I usually nag about what pose we'll come up with to show something special in our lives that year. "Do you have red and green shirts?"

"I just bought a red shirt," says Katie. She pulls it on over her black jersey.

Jeff rips off his navy shirt. He searches in his panniers, finds a green one, and pulls it on.

I get my camera ready, and the kids begin elaborate posing. They pretend to blow bad-smelling air from under their armpits toward the other's nose. Then they put their arms over each other's shoulder, but make faces at the camera.

"For a Christmas pose, how about a normal, human-imitating smile? You can fake it!"

The moment they cooperate, I snap as many shots as I can.

"Go team go! Thank you!" I say. The kids change their shirts again, and we pedal off.

My thoughts drift back to my encouraging Jeff about teaching. Teachers can't know if they have done a good job without determining whether students have learned something of value. Psychologist Carl Rogers said, "The basic idea behind teaching is to teach people what they need to know." Who gets to decide what students need to know?

I have reflected much on what I want my students to learn. I want them to approach literature with courage and curiosity, not defensiveness and defeat. I want them to connect the truths on the page with truths in their lives. Of course I want them to know where to put a comma and how to write concisely, but these mechanical skills are simply a means to their empowerment.

I ask my students what goals *they* have for my courses. Many of them respond, "I want to overcome my fear of speaking in front of a group." One of my assignments helps them attain that goal. In groups of three, students take responsibility for teaching the class one day. Doing this allows them to practice real world skills beyond those needed to interpret literature. They must cooperate with each other, plan a 90-minute session, know the subject inside and out, confer with me, present the activity engagingly to their peers, create and direct classroom activities, manage the time, evaluate themselves, and receive evaluations from their classmates as well as from me. In the workplace, the boss does not do the work with the employees passively watching. In my classroom, I let the students do the work, just as they will in their lives beyond the Ivory Tower. I conclude every semester with an anonymous course evaluation. I have never had less than ninety percent of the students answer "yes" to the question, "Shall I continue to have students participate in teaching groups?"

Teaching is not far removed from marketing. I may have to enlighten students about what they need and, by extension, therefore want. Aristotle said, "The more I want to get something done, the less I call it work." I introduce a new activity by saying, "Why am I asking you to do this? If I can't show why it is worth your time, then it probably isn't."

I wonder if my students have any idea that they are so important to me that I think about how to teach them well even when I am pedaling a bike in the mountains of Spain.

The paved road we're cycling continues to be almost empty. A few clouds are gathering, but rain doesn't seem to be threatening. Wind blows the bright wildflowers, sturdy yellow faces peering between the rock outcrops. When the road passes next to a slate cliff, imposing and dark, I get a sense of rock solid security. This mountain hasn't moved in a long time. I feel energized by the air's briskness. I wouldn't want to get stuck here overnight, but while the sun is shining, I love being on top of the world.

I ride slowly, and Katie catches up with me.

"What do you think about while you ride?" I ask her.

"Sometimes nothing, sometimes lots of stuff. Like will today be the day Dad breaks his record for shooting video the longest. What do you think about, Mom?"

"Usually the continuation of what we've just talked about. Since we were talking about teaching when Jeff changed my flat, I've been thinking about that. It's a subject I think a lot about anyway."

"Do you think you'll ever teach bike riding?" asks Katie.

"Myrtle laugh."

Katie and I switch places so she can ride ahead of me for a change. With her profile silhouetted in the sun, she looks like a petite woman, but conventional labels for life stages often don't mean much in relation to her.

When she was about three, we visited my sister and her family in Fairport, a suburb of Rochester. They had a West Highland Terrier named Snickers. He was an adorable ball of white fur dotted with warm dark eyes and topped with perky pink-lined ears. However, his high-pitched barking and excited running around were frightening to toddler Katie. One afternoon I was in the swimming pool and Katie was walking on the deck. Snickers came bouncing and barking over to her. Intimidated, Katie started backing away from him. From my spot in the pool, I could not restrain Snickers, but I knew I could catch Katie. She took one more step back and landed in the pool. I grabbed her the instant she hit the water and with a big grin, said, "Hi, honey. What are you doing?"

Without missing a beat, she said, "Looking for fish."

This afternoon, as I ride down single track with lots of brush on either side, I negotiate a sharp right turn and discover Katie's bike lying on the ground to the left of the trail. Katie is on her back in a marshy mush of weeds and reeds. She does not appear to be in pain. What can I ask other than, "Looking for fish?"

"Eeew, Mom. Help me up."

I lean over and give her a pull.

"You're OK, aren't you?"

"Nothing's broken."

"When you fell, was it a 'wow' or a 'yikes'?"

"It was a 'yuck."

She's pretty muddy.

"Remember when your soccer coach had all the girls roll in the mud so they wouldn't be afraid to get their new uniforms dirty?"

"That was fun. This is stinky. And these blackberries have prickers."

Joe catches up to us and exudes sympathy to Katie. We pour water from our bottles that she uses to rinse her hands and legs. Then Joe rides ahead and radios Jeff to wait for us. I watch the trail behind us while Katie changes, and I think about the origin of our family's dialect when it comes to "wow" and "yikes."

When Jeff was six, Joe was having his new recording studio built as an addition to our house. Steve, a neighbor, did some of the site preparation work in his Bobcat. When I got home late from teaching one day, Joe told me that Steve had invited Jeff to climb into the empty scoop, which he slowly raised. Then he carefully drove the cat from the site up to our driveway. Jeff listened as Joe told me about the adventure. I turned and asked Jeff, "What was it like? Did you say 'Wow'?"

"No, Mom," he said with his eyes wide, "It wasn't a 'wow.' It was a 'yikes'!"

West of Rabanal, I hope to experience a "wow." I

have been looking forward to participating in the tradition at the iron cross where pilgrims leave something tangible, usually in honor of something intangible. Some bring a picture of a deceased friend or relative who had wanted to do the Camino but not been able to. Other pilgrims tack, tape or tie personal mementoes on the oak beam that supports the cross, perhaps a bandana or poem or *concha.* The most common contribution is a stone left at the base of the cross. Some pilgrims carry stones with them for miles before leaving them there; others simply grab one nearby and add it to the pile. Before we left home, I collected four small pieces of sandstone from our yard and gave one to each member of the family. I hoped we could carry the stones as we rode the Camino and then add them to the centuries' collection at the base of the iron cross. I liked the symbolism of our leaving a little bit of our home at this site on the other side of the world.

Early in the afternoon, we come around a curve in the Camino, and there is the cross. The cross itself is not very large, maybe two feet tall, but it is mounted on a larger-than-life wooden timber at the top of a 20' high mound. A road passes near the spot, and a busload of tourists is just leaving. A group of Italian road bikers stands by a large van carrying their gear. They troop up the hill to look closely at the cross and drop their stones.

We wait until they leave, but other pilgrims arrive, bunching up at this landmark. An unspoken etiquette emerges. One or two pilgrims climb the narrow path up the hill to look at the array of objects, notes, and flags posted there, and many leave something. Their friends snap a picture. After they come down, the next set of pilgrims take their turn. It reminds me of mountain climbers photographing their mates at the summit.

I am first in our family to go up. Other people are waiting, so I can't take too long. I see snapshots and notes that wrench my heart. In Spanish, one says, "This is for you, Mama." A small photo of a relatively young man has this inscribed on it: "You didn't live to complete the Camino, but now you are here." I am thankful I don't need to leave a photograph or note. I lean down and carefully place my little piece of sandstone from my corner of the earth on top of larger rocks near where I am standing. This is my moment to be part of this tradition. Joe takes his turn, and I photograph him setting a California stone on the Spanish mound.

"Did you put it next to mine?" I ask him.

"Which one was yours?" he says.

"The one that looked like yours."

"Yes, I did."

"Your turn, Jeff," I say.

"I don't think I'll do it." I suspect he feels self-conscious about approaching the cross in front of an audience, and he's not caught up in the power of the tradition.

"Are you sure? You've carried that stone for hundreds of miles."

"I don't think I will either," says Katie.

"What would Nick and Lisa do?" I ask.

"They would generously give their stones to their parents," says Katie.

"And they'd take pictures of the parents tossing their stones for them."

Holding hands, Joe and I go back up. Jeff has trained the video camera on us, and Katie is ready with my still camera.

"Let's toss the stones together." We throw them in unison, just as we've thrown in our lot together. We wave at our creations, busy capturing their parents in a sentimental moment, a celebration of our journey together on this Camino, in this life. I have Joe to thank for so much that brings me happiness. I squeeze his hand. As we climb down, Joe says little. When he gets choked up, he grows quiet. I reach for the kleenex.

Joe fears the next part of our ride might become a "yikes." West of the iron cross, the Camino shares a little traveled highway that descends about six hundred meters in fifteen kilometers. That's almost two thousand feet in about ten miles. Road signs warn trucks about the steep grade, and our guidebook reports that every year some cyclists go too fast, lose control and crash to their deaths.

As we stand at the top of this descent, Joe announces in his sternest voice, "This looks like a fun downhill, but it's dangerous. I want everyone to promise to brake regularly."

"I will," I say.

"Jeff, will you check the brakes?" says Joe.

He does. I'm not sure if he and Katie are convinced of the potential danger here or only acting as if they are.

Joe says, "I will go first." Eyeing Jeff, he lays down the law. "Nobody is to pass me."

"I'll go last," I say. Joe heads out, then Jeff, then Katie.

This paved road is not scary like the rutted, rocky, unridable cliffs we've descended. I'm not worried at all about the steepness of the descent. My brakes work.

Sunshine has always given me confidence, and the brisk air of the mountains gives me energy. I make myself wait not because of nerves, but because I want to set my own pace. The further back I am, the more leeway I will have.

Joe, Jeff and Katie become specks on the mountainside below. I'm an Olympic ski jumper at the top of the chute, and I can't wait to go. I push off.

What sweet coasting bliss! Spain, thank you for another empty mountain road. It's just me and my bike, me and myself.

I swoop in wide arcs, cutting serpentine swaths. I am at Heavenly Valley, gliding from mogul to mogul. With this slope beneath my skis, I lean left, then right. My heart pounds and I gulp the rushing air.

Then, like Walter Mitty, I become a glider pilot. I am surrounded by the swooshing roar of the air my plane cuts through.

I should keep my eyes on the road, but I sneak a long look at the mountain's panorama of shiny slate cliffs highlighted with deep green foliage.

My tires pick up a rhythm that matches my exhilarated pulse. I hum Joe's Latin-flavored "Highway One." I am cruisin'.

The temperature changes as I slice through pockets of cool air and then warm air rising from the valley. I'm swimming in a lake with cold spots and hot spots. Then I'm not in the lake, but *on* it. I'm piloting a sailboat that has quit slamming against the waves and has leapt atop the white caps, planing smoothly across the crests. Then I fly above the water and become a gull, soaring with wings outstretched.

I am intoxicated with the rush of this ride. Let freedom ring. There is no drug as good as reality.

How long does the descent take? As long as making love or music, when time doesn't pass at all.

At the bottom of the mountain, a tiny village hugs a meandering river. A quaint hotel looks more like a Swiss chalet than a Spanish resort. The river is dammed, creating a swimming hole with an inviting green lawn beside it. Sunbathers lounge on colorful towels. I suggest we stay there. I want to prolong our connection with this spot. But Mr. Practical points out that the afternoon is still young. We keep going.

After coasting for so many miles, pushing the pedals seems like unfamiliar and unwanted work. I grow sweaty and bored. This virtually deserted paved road that I would have found pleasurable to ride yesterday seems dull compared to my free sailing down the mountain.

We cycle through one tiny village after another, some of them containing more dilapidated structures than habitable ones. In California, these falling apart sheds would be fixer-uppers on the market for a half million dollars each.

To make this stretch more interesting, I cruise in front of Jeff and tell him, "My turn to lead for a while."

I focus on my legs and balance and breathing. Time and I are now moving slowly.

Jeff beeps me on the radio. "Didn't you want to stop at that monument to the cyclist? You just passed it."

I did? Huh? Whoa!

"How far back is it?" I say, turning around.

"Just a little bit."

Bo and lehold, in my petulant self-absorption I blindly pedaled right by one of the monuments I'd found intriguing before we started the trip and which I had described to the family. To Jeff's credit, he had obviously listened.

I turn back and find him starting to climb up onto the monument. It's a replica of a bike made of rebar and topped with an artistic representation of a pilgrim's hat.

"What's special about it?" Jeff asks as he starts climbing up it.

"It's a tribute to a German cyclist who died on the Camino. His friend built it in his memory."

Jeff gets down.

I snap a picture at the moment when a line of horseback riders alongside the road passes in my field of vision framed by the bike's back wheel. Are they pilgrims en route to Santiago? I don't know, but their presence, behind this monument, reminds me that although modes of transportation change over time, going west to Santiago, or to San Francisco, or to the Yukon gold fields – that quest endures whether the adventurers travel on foot, bicycle, or horseback.

We finally pedal into Ponferrada, our destination for the night. After cleaning up, eager to search for possible restaurants, we walk a few blocks to the square. I savor the cooling dusk and slight breeze, as soft on my cheek as a butterfly kiss. Because it is still early for Spanish dinner, we suspect we won't find any restaurants that are open, but we feel too hungry not to look, just in case. I'm delighted that we find one option, El Templo de Cerveza.

"Let's go worship," says Jeff.

"I'm a believer," says Katie.

Food sounds heavenly to me, too. Here in the Temple of Beer, as elsewhere, the prices are very reasonable. We order the usual *Menu del Dia* and inhale the dinner for a total bill of about forty dollars. I drink wine, but Joe and the kids honor the *Templo* and drink beer. Amen.

As we stroll back to the hotel, I notice that the evening is almost chilly. Mounted on poles near the sidewalk, flags flap and slap in the breeze. I wonder if the mountains we are entering will be as cool and wet as the Pyrennées, where we began.

TAKING THE HEAT

"What time is it?" I ask Joe, who's just gotten up.

"It's 7:00. I'm going to shave. Stay in bed a little longer if you want to."

As I lie there, I recall waking up in Belorado, more than a week ago, relieved that the window was still dark. The sun was not up, so I didn't need to get up either. I curled deeper under the covers, but I could not ignore a mysterious tap-tap-tapping on the road below. No ravens were quothing "Never more." Sometimes the tapping sounded loud and jumbled together, sometimes soft and subtle. It seemed to be moving past the window. It couldn't be the footsteps of animals being herded down the street, because I didn't hear cowbells, moo's or bah's. Then I smiled. It must be pilgrims, even before first light, tapping their walking sticks as they went. I'm glad we don't get started that early.

Most days we eat breakfast at a café-bar (café in the morning, bar in the evening). This morning we revisit the Temple of Beer. In the sunlight, the place looks different. I'm sure we do too. I love the huge, fluffy, still-warm croissants, café con leche, and orange juice. Maybe it's because Valencia and oranges are synonymous that Spain has the freshest, most delicious orange juice I've ever tasted. Virtually every café has a Zumit machine that looks as if a

Disney cartoonist designed it. The bartender inserts oranges in the top of the Zumit, the machine cuts them open and then gives them the squeeze.

During breakfast, Joe says, "What comes down must go up." Yesterday's descent, he warns us, will be more than balanced by several ascents today.

Pleasant as breakfast always is, we don't dawdle. Morning mist is our friend.

We pedal out of the center of town and pass a public park on our right.

"Ramps!" Jeff calls out.

We turn in and see several huge metal ramps. They have been heavily graffitied.

"Do you want to try them out?" I ask.

"Not on this bike, and not with panniers and racks."

"This seems like a great opportunity for you to have some of your kind of riding fun."

"These ramps are for BMX bikes. Katie, your bike is the smallest. Can I ride yours?"

She gives a thumbs up. He removes her panniers while she takes off her handlebar bag. At this hour, we are the only human souls around. Jeff gets on Katie's bike and bunny hops onto one of the ramps. He begins a pattern of back and forth swoops. He pedals only a few times, but builds up huge momentum. My boy has legs. At the top of each side of the symmetrical ramp, he leaps up and swings his bike around in mid-air, changing directions to land back down on the ramp. The metal clangs and clunks each time he lands.

"I've watched Jeff do this a million times," I say to Katie standing next to me, "but I've never seen a metal ramp before. The racket this makes is kind of unnerving."

"It's my bike. I hope he doesn't break it," she says.

I'm so glad she feels this way. My heart soars along with Jeff's leaps.

On one wheel, Jeff jumps down from the ramp and rides a few of the other slides and tables. Then he cruises over to us.

"These metal ramps are really sketchy," he says. "There's no traction, and the metal has too much give."

"In that case, I'm especially glad you've finished riding them," I say, standing up to put a period on that comment.

As Katie and Jeff put her panniers back on, I ask him, "How do you turn in mid-air? You're like a diver who leaves the board and then twists and twirls. I can't fathom how a person does that."

"I practiced," he says.

"Only on the days you ate," says Katie, quoting Dr. Suzuki, founder of the violin method Katie learned from.

We all get back on our bikes and cycle out of Ponferrada. I am always struck by how suddenly a Spanish town transitions into countryside. Adobe houses share walls, connected side by side, until a final wall defines the end of the town and the border of a field, often enclosed with a flimsy fence that functions well enough to keep a few sheep, goats or a cow enclosed.

This morning's stretch of the Camino is like the others in that it never stays the same for long. It is a tractor trail for a few miles, then a village lane, then a path next to a highway. I have concluded that the surface of the trail – sandy or rocky, cobblestone or paved – is usually the key to its difficulty. So far, a paved uphill has been tiring but not as challenging as a very rocky downhill, which takes nerves and skill, both of which I still need more of.

I am pleased when Joe reports that our guidebook advises cyclists on the next section to take the road instead of the hiking path. The heat is building up, so I feel relieved that we will have an easy surface to ride. I remember all too well the hot endurance test on a rocky narrow trail a couple of days ago.

However, I soon see I'm in for a scorching reassessment of that notion. As we pedal uphill, the blissfully smooth black asphalt exacerbates the heat. We are making a long steady climb up pavement that absorbs the sun, turns up the temperature, and then expels it upwards toward us. Traffic is almost nonexistent, probably because most drivers, like two we have seen, are taking siestas in their trucks parked in the shade of roadside trees. Unlike them, we truck on.

I shift to a gear that allows me to make progress without burning so many calories that I have to stop to re-oxygenate every ten yards. Sweat cascades down my forehead, my back and my belly. I remember learning in seventh grade that evaporation causes cooling. This sweat is not evaporating. It is drenching me in a warm sogginess. The road curves its way up the mountain, so we cannot see ahead to get a sense of how much longer the uphill, stovetop conditions will continue.

I radio to Team K-W, "Let's stop for lunch whenever we see enough shade for us all to fit under."

"Roger and out," says Jeff.

After what has probably been only a few minutes but has felt like an hour, I pedal up to where I spy Jeff sitting under a shade tree. Perfect. Katie and Joe join us and we pull our picnics out.

"I think this is an Anne Lamott climb," I say.

"What's that?" asks Katie.

"She's the author of a book called *Bird by Bird.* She chose the title because of her older brother. He had postponed a big school project, something your brother would never do."

"That's right Katie, I'm always perfect."

"He was supposed to make a bird book, but the night before it was due, he hadn't even started. He asked their dad, 'How can I get this done?' The dad answered, 'Bird by bird.'"

"So what is it here? Mountain by mountain?" asks Katie.

"The great cellist Yo Yo Ma says he learned the Bach Cello Suites by practicing two measures a day. So we can climb these hills bit by bit, pedal by pedal, not getting overwhelmed by the whole."

"I try not to think about the physical work," says Joe.

"So let's make the climb bird by bird, without thinking about the birds."

"This is getting awfully complicated," says Jeff. "Let's just ride."

For Jeff, "just riding" is easy. For the rest of us, it's a different story. I say, "Here's a tale I tell my students. It's the Myth of Sisyphus. Try saying that three times fast."

Jeff and Katie start reciting "Myth of Sisyphus," which quickly becomes "Myth of Thithyphuth."

"Sisyphus angered Zeus, the most powerful of the ancient Greek Gods. Zeus decided that killing Sisyphus would let him get off too easy. Instead, he assigned him eternal, meaningless work. He had to push a huge rock up a hill. After it rolled back down, which it always did, he would repeat the process – forever."

"Um, he thought about birds as he pushed the rock?" says the Mistress of Sarcasm.

"Zeus controlled Sisyphus' fate, but not his mind. Imagine this: Sisyphus leaned into that boulder, enjoying the exercise as a way to buff up. He savored feeling the roughness of the rock on his palms. He flexed his biceps and clenched his leg muscles, bulging from the effort. At the top, he said, 'Check out this rock. It's going to careen down hill, smashing and crashing in an awesome display of gravity. It's a show worth repeating, and I'm going to do it again.' Sisyphus wins."

"So Mom is trying to say we can turn around and coast back down this mountain and then buff up climbing it again," says Katie. "I'll wait here for you."

"I'm trying to say that instead of getting too focused on the elevation change and heat and sweat, we can think about our incremental accomplishments. We just made it up that steep, black pavement in the hottest part of the day, so hurray for us. And I challenge everybody to come up with a positive thought or story to share the next time we stop."

When we get back on the blacktop, I realize my saying we had made the climb in the hottest part of the day may have been wrong. It feels even hotter now. But I'll try to think of something positive to share.

When searching for the positive, I think of my dad. I never saw him depressed even though he came of age in the Depression. After his father lost his real estate business, Dad played it safe. He sold insurance. His business grew from a single desk he rented in the corner of another business, to an entire office, to several branches. He was never wealthy, but in the important parts of life, he would have been the first to say he was rich.

So are we. Money can't buy the family bonds that are being cemented as we push ourselves and each other to succeed on this adventure.

My thoughts are interrupted when Joe calls out gruffly

from behind me, "Rest." I turn around to see him get off his bike, drop it on the ground, and collapse next to it. Oh my God! I call on my radio to Jeff who's out in front, "Hold up." I throw my bike on the side of the road and hurry down to Joe. He is so weak he needs help taking his backpack off.

Jeff arrives on the scene. "Wow, Dad," he says. Katie says nothing.

Joe's sweat has soaked not only his blue cotton shirt, but right through his backpack and much of its contents. He lies down, panting, barely able to speak.

"Do you feel nauseous?" I ask him, terrified that he might be having a heart attack.

"No," he grunts. "Hot."

"Have some water," I say. My mind races. What should I do? Why did I never take a Red Cross course? I'm helpless, useless.

"Can't," he says. "Out."

I look at his bike. His three large water bottles are empty. Almost every village has a fountain where we refill our water supply, but in the last town we passed, the fountain wasn't functioning. I still have one full bottle, so it hadn't mattered much to me. Joe hadn't said anything about it.

"Here, Dad," says Jeff, offering one of his bottles.

While Joe drinks, I say as casually and quietly as I can, "Jeff, why don't you grab a book or two from Dad's panniers? I bet you'd hardly notice the extra weight." Without comment, he removes three of them and slides them into his panniers. Katie grabs a few items, as do I.

Joe appears oblivious to us. He leans back on one elbow, not quite lying on the ground, but not holding himself in a sitting position, either. He is silent and still, his gray face showing nothing but self-absorbed exhaustion. He looks older than his 53 years. His only motion is taking occasional long drinks of water. Instead of Jeff-Katie banter, there is quiet. I'm glad the kids can't hear the nervous pounding in my chest. They probably are dealing with their own fear. Our anchor, our central cedar pole, our captain, my partner, is almost limp, almost helpless, almost done. I don't want to stare at him, but I must. He is all that matters.

After a while, Joe sits up. He says, "I ran out of water. I was just beat."

"The heat makes this harder than our rides at home," I say, struggling to be conversational when my adrenaline is racing.

Joe doesn't even respond.

"Take your time, keep drinking," I say. There's no level ground here, much less a shaded spot, where we can sit and relax together while he composes himself. We're on the edge of the road. The kids and I continue to stand, awkwardly.

I look again at Joe's drawn face and sense his determination to minimize what has just happened. I know him. His pride is offended that he is the one who collapsed, he is the one who hasn't made it up the hill.

I'm not surprised when he slowly stands and says, "Let's go."

"Are you sure? Take a few more minutes," I say.

"Yeah, Dad," says Jeff, "we can wait 'til you're ready."

"I'm ready," he says.

For the rest of the climb, I frequently say I want to rest. We stop often.

Dread clutches at my throat. I am pretending things are now OK. Is that what we are all doing? Joe looks like he's been through the wringer. At the next fountain we come to, we refill our water bottles. I don't ask if anyone came up with a positive story, as I think we would agree it would be that Dad Didn't Die.

I try to focus on the exquisite landscape with its gray slate outcroppings highlighted with delicate yellow and purple wildflowers. But even with the beauty surrounding us beneath this stunning blue sky, I can't slough off the fear I felt when "heat" became another four-letter word. As it was happening, I pushed back the terror of dealing with the "what-ifs." Now, imprisoned in my solitary brain, I can't stop thinking about them.

What if Joe had completely passed out, had a heart attack or a stroke? Here in the countryside, where and how could I have found help? We are in the middle of nowhere. We are only us. Would I have left Jeff and Katie to stay with Joe, and ridden my bike in a random search for someone who could contact a doctor? Or sent Jeff to speed his way to wherever to find help? And even if we found someone willing and capable of coming to our aid, how could I have explained what happened? My Spanish is fine for casual conversations, but there's no way I feel competent to speak on Joe's behalf in critical decision-making.

I don't want to imagine my life without the love of my life. I break out in another sweat. The kids need their Dad. Our fates might have just changed forever, but here we are, pedaling along. We have dodged a life-and-death bullet. I cowered when the shadow of mortality crossed Joe's face, before it slipped away into the searing sun. We are the luckiest family in the world.

Heat put Joe to the test. With water, will power and lots of rest stops, he passed the test. As for having to rescue him in a medical emergency, I hope that's a test I never need to take, no matter what language it's in.

Very slowly, our entourage finally reaches the ridge top, where arrows direct us to a trail that is relatively smooth and hard packed. Ahead of us I see hill after hill. We ascend the next one and then find ourselves on a road with little traffic. It is the "old road." High above, the new freeway crosses over us. What the old and new road have in common is the general direction – uphill.

As the afternoon wears on, my psyche and body know they have been working harder and longer than even my improved stamina can comfortably handle. Our destination is a mountaintop town called O Cebreiro, shown in photos as a mist-shrouded, medieval-looking village of low stone buildings with slate roofs.

"How much farther?" I make myself not ask. This day has already lasted too long. Revision: I am relieved we have lasted this long.

We cover the kilometers slowly, humbled by gravity's grip. The road is not much traveled, but a solo car coming toward us turns on its lights. Yikes, let's get there.

Finally, we see a sign, "Cebreiro .7." Whew, only 7/10 of a kilometer to go. All uphill, true. And it is getting pretty dark, true. But we are nearly there, yes.

We pedal farther and farther, always uphill. The kids are quiet. I finally say to Joe, hoping the kids won't overhear my anxiety, "Is it just because I'm tired, or does this seem like more than 7/10 of a kilometer?"

"I think somebody put a period in front of the seven. It's really seven kilometers."

There is nothing to do but deal with one more bird.

We finally spot O Cebreiro, a small cluster of buildings, not really a town. We see a handful of cars, and a herdful of tourist buses. Uh-oh.

We enter the inns, one by one. There aren't many, and all of them are full. An employee sympathetic to our plight offers to loan us pieces of cardboard to put over the dirt to sleep on next to the building. We have no sleeping bags or even warm jackets.

We stand in the hallway of one inn, unsure of what to try next. A wide entrance to the adjacent bar shows a good-sized crowd of people, a roaring fireplace, and a tall, cheerful woman with light brown hair tending the bar. She returns my smile. I step in, briefly explain our dilemma, and ask her if she can suggest any other place to stay, possibly farther along the Camino. We are at the summit, so maybe we can coast really fast, breaking our rule about not riding in the dark, so we can find beds for the night. She graciously calls the only hotel in the next village, and it is booked solid.

I can't believe this is happening. We have money, but there is no lodging to purchase. How have we gotten ourselves AND OUR CHILDREN into this fix? I can't wrap my head around the idea that we are helpless, alone, and stuck not between a rock and a hard place, but between freezing and freezing. We have deluded ourselves into thinking that we are competent, responsible people. I am humbled for the second time today by our vulnerability and by my arrogant notion of control over our fate.

Then before our eyes the bartender is transformed into the Angel of the Camino. She calls a friend who runs a hotel in the town of Pedrafita, about six hundred feet below us. We had cycled right past it, but hadn't even thought about stopping there, as our goal was O Cebreiro. Did he have a room? Yes. She asks him to send someone to drive up to get us. She offers to keep our bikes in her garage. We will not have to ride down to the hotel in the dark, nor be Sisyphus and climb back up in the morning. We ask the angel her name, and she says "Irene." When we take our bikes to her garage, we remark about the acoustic guitar case we see there. She explains that her husband plays, and she loves listening to him. When we get home, we will send her *The Waltz of the Whippoorwill*, one of Joe's CDs that features his guitar playing.

Our safe, soft beds that night are the most appreciated of the trip. We will make reservations ahead from now on. I can imagine Grandpa Florida nodding. Insurance is a good thing.

IT'S NOT OVER

"Joe, I know I can't live without you, but I'd like to think I can buy a dress on my own."

"I could help if there are any language issues," he says.

"That's exactly the reason why I want to go solo."

"What are the kids doing?" he asks.

"They're exploring the town together and will meet us for dinner."

"Have fun," he says, looking a bit forlorn. I head out.

We expect to make it to Santiago in the next two or three days, so if there's anything I especially want to do before we get there, I better do it soon. Now is the perfect time. We're in Sarria, a mountainside town much larger than the villages we've been passing through.

I'm sick of my two t-shirts and shorts, one for cycling and the other for non-cycling. So, I'll venture onto the retail trail. I will buy a nonwrinkleable dress that I can stash in my panniers during the day, but wear when we go out to dinner, which we do every night. And I also want to have the experience of relying on my Spanish, by myself.

This town does not have a department store, but little shops selling women's clothing abound. As soon as I enter one, I'm aware of how odd I look. Most Spanish women wear dresses. Here I am in denim shorts, my light blue sweat-wicking high tech cycling t-shirt, and tennis shoes.

My "purse" is my black boxy handlebar bag.

Hopefully a smile can help make up for my queerness, but this is not a place accustomed to tourists like me. I am on my own.

The clerk in the first store is friendly. I explain what I'm looking for, and she points me to a rack. The dresses are much fancier and pricier than what I have in mind. I thank her and leave. I visit more stores, try on several dresses, and slide into shopping mode. Spanish interactions here are more formal than they are in Mexican culture, and I suspect my limited vocabulary makes me seem less courteous than I'd like to be, but it's becoming easier to relax and chat. By the fourth store, I am having fun. There must be a bond among women shopping for a new dress. The clerks seem to mirror my enjoyment in what I have decided is a universal female pleasure.

In the last women's clothing store on the main street I spot a dress that looks a bit skimpy, but otherwise perfect. My "I want to get *some*thing" voice is outweighing my practical inclinations. The polyester black fabric, washable and smunchable without wrinkling, is brightened by a pattern of little red roses. The hemline flows from high to low, and a small ruffle along the bottom mirrors a ruffle on the top. It has spaghetti straps and a black lining. It would be perfect to wear at formal gigs.

It is reasonably priced, the tag says it was "Made in Spain," and it fits great, or will when I get a strapless bra. Hmm. I don't know how to say either "bra" or "strapless," but a quick pantomime makes my need clear to the clerk. Most unfortunately, this shop does not sell such a garment. Still, I buy the dress, and the clerk directs me to the shoe repair store a couple of blocks away. Shoe repair store?

I find it right where she said it would be. I peek in the

window before I go in. It's a narrow shop. Boxes of shoes are stacked on shelves from floor to ceiling along the right wall. Boxes of bras are stacked along the left wall. Then I have a revelation. The sizes will not be in inches, and I have no idea what size to ask for. I don't want to ask the clerk, a young man, to give me an estimate. I need crisis counseling for shyness.

Sassy Self: For heaven's sake, break out of your comfort zone, you wuss.

Sissy Self: I think the dress does not really require that I wear a bra.

Sassy: Scaredy cat, scaredy cat. Grow up.

Sissy: I'll wait here until another woman goes in, and see what she does.

Sassy: How many customers seem to be around?

Sissy: Well, maybe someone will come along.

Self: Hmm.

I go in. I ask for size "medium" and he gives me a bra to try on that is too small. The second try is close enough, so I pay him and scurry off.

Years ago, I explained to Joe that when I ask, "How do you like my new dress?" I am not really asking how he likes it. I am asking for validation.

When I get back to our room, he spies the bags I'm carrying.

"Congratulations! Can I see it?"

I have never known a man who can comment on a dress unless a woman is wearing it, so I put it on. When I model it for Joe, he says, "I like it. It looks great, and those ruffles seem Spanish."

An hour later, nobody laughs as we walk to dinner when I put my rain jacket on over my dress to keep warm in the chilly evening.

The next day we cycle deeper into the northwestern corner of Spain. It is called Galicia, not accidentally similar to Gaelic. Many inhabitants have the fair skin and light eyes typical of the Irish, and the traditional music features bagpipes and whistles. The place names sound only vaguely Spanish. With the dictator Franco long gone, regional idioms are allowed once again. We have reserved a hotel in Pal do Reis, whose name seems a variant of Palacio de Reyes, or Palace of the Kings.

Today the Camino is taking us past one small dairy farm after another. We are light years away from the neat lush vineyards of Logroño, the expansive wheat fields of the rolling plains, and the urban sophistication of Burgos and León. Joe says the pleasure of discovering the constantly changing landscapes makes him forget the hard work it takes to cycle through them. Here the narrow lane is rutted and muddy. As for the many fresh cow patties, Katie holds her nose and asks, "Do you have a gas mask I can borrow, Mom?"

Uh-oh. A small herd of cow patty sources ambles toward us. A young man walks behind them, holding a long stick and urging them along. Fences border the dirt road on both sides. There's no choice but to stop as close to the fence as we can, put our feet down in the muck, and hope the cows, who are amazingly huge this up-close and personal, are friendly.

Joe calls out "Good afternoon" to the cowherd, who nods. We 21st Century cyclists wait to let a man and his herd, who could be from any century, have the right of way. *Buen Camino.*

A flash of black and white swoops by in the trees to my right. Joe calls out, "Hoopoe, Marty!" He captured the scene on his camera. The bird is long gone, but Joe rewinds the tape to show us. As a music producer, Joe knows that "tapes don't lie," and indeed, this clearly shows a hoopoe, large and remarkable not only for its name, but also its head topped by a Mohawk-like black comb.

In the yard of almost every farmhouse, a tall, rectangular structure sits on stilts three or four feet off the ground. Some of the stilts look like mushrooms. What are these things for? Then it dawns on me. There must be rats, and these must be storage containers for corn or grains, kept safe from the rodents' appetite.

The Camino abruptly morphs from a country lane to the main street of Pal do Reis. It descends from east to west. We have reserved rooms in a hotel at the west end of town. Before coasting down to it, we spot a bike shop.

We value the axiom that luck favors the prepared. We have been hoping to pick up an adapter for our tires so that if we happen to pass a gas station (which we never do), we can use their air compressor to inflate our tires higher than Jeff has been able to with his hand pump. A tire kept at high pressure is less likely to get a flat. Most of the villages the Camino traverses are too small to have either a gas station or a bike shop, but Pal do Reis is larger. Jeff also wants to refill his supply of duct tape. The latter is his choice for number eleven in the Ten Essentials Kit his Scout troop insists every boy carry on every outing, things like a pocket knife, compass, map, flashlight, and basic first aid supplies.

Duct tape of course gets its name from its original purpose, to hold together ducts and pipes in plumbing/heating/industrial settings. Now it holds the world together. In the bike shop it is sold in packaging labeled "Duck" tape featuring a picture of a mallard. I wonder how many Spaniards have questioned why crazy

Americans named the tape after a bird. As we make our purchases, I explain the duck/duct trivia to Jesús, the shop owner. We chat for a while, and he wishes us a good conclusion of our trip. We are only about sixty kilometers from Santiago.

We coast down hill to our hotel, check in, clean up, and then meet to search for a restaurant that might already be open for dinner.

"Shall we ride our bikes, or do you want to walk?" I ask.

"I've been riding my bike quite a bit lately," Katie says. "I'll walk."

"I'll ride," says Jeff, "but how 'bout on your bike, Dad?"

Joe and I walk with Katie, and Jeff powers the Motiv up the hill. We spot a restaurant on the left side of the street whose long waiting line suggests it might be good and about to open for the evening. Jeff pulls the handlebars up and wheelies on the back tire. And then, he stops suddenly, awkwardly, unexpectedly.

Jeff leans over, and for a moment I think he might be hurt. He picks something up from the ground, turns around and shows us.

"The crank broke!" he says. That's the metal piece connecting the pedal to the sprocket.

"Could duct tape hold it together?" I ask.

"No way."

"Could duck tape do it?"

"No way."

Slowly I realize that this is no joking matter. Joe's bike has become unridable. Could our trip be ended prematurely, so near to Santiago, due to a mechanical problem?

Aware that it is almost nine o'clock, I say with little

conviction, "Maybe Jesús is still in his bike shop? Maybe he'll have a crank that will fit?" Both possibilities seem as remote as our bumping into Santiago himself.

Joe says, "Jeff, run up to the shop as fast as your young self can go. If his door is open even a crack, knock and go in. I'll walk the bike up and meet you there."

"There's no point in all of us going," I say. "Katie and I can get a place in the waiting line for the restaurant, so when you come back, we can all eat," I say.

A half hour passes. The line advances slowly, and still there is no sign of the men.

"Maybe that's good," I suggest. "If the shop were closed, then they would have come back right away."

"Could be, or maybe it's closed and they're walking around trying to find another one."

After an hour, Katie and I are seated. I have asked for a table for four, but there are only two of us. This is awkward.

As the waiter hands me a menu, Jeff and Joe enter the restaurant. They are smiling. This is the way things happen in Hollywood – and in Pal do Reis?

Not only was Jesús still at the store, he had an identical crank. He sold it to them and installed it for about fifteen euros. We would have paid fifty for it, or a hundred and fifty!

I lift my wine glass and we toast Jesús.

In the morning the drizzle doesn't dampen our spirits. We don our rain jackets. The hotelkeeper tells us the Camino will leave the paved road shortly after we get out of town, in less than a kilometer, and we should watch for it on the right.

I cycle in my usual spot behind Jeff, who's in the lead.

Water on the pavement seems to have loosened the oil on the surface, and I smell a mixture of cleansing raindrops with stinky automobile detritus. At least we'll soon return to the trail. I wonder whether we'll make Santiago today. I both do and don't want to get there. This journey is exhausting and exhilarating, terribly hard and tremendously inspiring. Our family may never feel so much like a team again.

"Marty! Watch out!" Joe yells.

On my left, an old red sedan skids by on the slick wet pavement. It comes to a stop about thirty feet from me. The driver seems confused. He sits for a moment, looks around, restarts the car, and then drives on. Fortunately, no other cars come by.

I turn around to see Joe with his arm around Katie's shoulders. She is crying. I pedal back to them.

In uneven phrases, gulping between tears, she blurts out what happened.

"I was right behind Dad. Then this car came past me. Then it started skidding. It completely spun around. I thought it was going to hit Dad. I thought he was going to …." More tears. "Then it came right at me. It came so close I could feel the wind."

We all hug, a life grip. Katie regains her composure, and my feelings race from panic to celebration, terror to jubilation. While I had been contemplating the feel-good subtleties of our arrival, or not, in Santiago today, fifty feet behind me Joe and Katie almost lost their lives.

If the driver had been going one mile per hour faster, the tires had been slightly more bald, or the roadway a little more slippery, this brief moment of fate could have made an ending too terrible to imagine.

I am scared. I am enraged. I am thankful.

I call Jeff on the radio. "Dad and Katie almost had an accident, but they're OK. Wait for us where you are, and we'll catch up to you."

We ride up the curving hill and spy Jeff, a worried boy. We tell him briefly and then pedal hard, eager to get as far away from this road as we can. To our relief, the Camino soon heads off to the right, as the hotelkeeper said it would. A broken crank no longer seems so threatening to our success, and the muddy, rocky, rutted, car-free Camino trail could not feel more welcoming. I remind myself to breathe.

The drizzle changes to big fat raindrops, so we pull out our shower caps, bright yellow waterproof coverings that stretch over our panniers. We pedal through the farm-studded countryside until we come to a group of pilgrims huddling together. We have noticed the trail is becoming more crowded the closer we get to Santiago. In fact, walking pilgrims can get their credentials validated if they've walked a minimum of one hundred kilometers; for cyclists, the minimum is two hundred. The stamped credential is the badge of courage and accomplishment, the tangible proof that a pilgrim has made it all the way. We, of course, are riding the whole Camino, about eight hundred kilometers. But this jam isn't caused by the number of pilgrims. It's caused by the fact that more than a dozen of them are all standing still on this narrow trail. They seem to be looking at something to the left of the path. Then we see it too.

Fifteen feet from us stands a large black and white dairy cow. She has just given birth. The umbilical cord dangles from her bloody vulva, and her wet calf lies in the dirt. Jeff and Katie make faces and in unison assess the situation: "Eeeeuw."

"Kiddoes, we are seeing a newborn calf!" I whisper.

"Disgusting," says Katie.

"Gross," says Jeff.

This nativity scene has no cuddly lambs or sweet-smelling hay, no leafy bower where this cow could have chosen to have her calf in private, protected from chilly drizzle and human eyes. Instead, she had only a small barnyard enclosed by a board fence that might have once been painted white. The calf's side, belly and spindly legs are dirty. The sky is dripping.

The scene still feels holy. I tell the kids, "I think the mother must be experienced. Look at her lick the calf to warm him and stimulate his circulation. See how she nudges him and then starts to walk away. She wants her baby to stand up and follow her."

The calf tries to push up on spindly legs. We hold our breath. The calf topples over.

The mother repeats her encouragement. We wait, we cross our fingers, we want to applaud the little creature's first steps, but again the calf wobbles and collapses.

The raindrops get bigger and closer together. Same for my goose bumps.

I say, "The calf looks healthy, and this is a good mama. Let's hope that's enough, and let's move along." I do not say, "Let's hope no out-of-control red cars crash into their lives."

Joe puts a plastic bag around the camera to protect it from the rain, and he glances at me. Is it raindrops or tears on my cheeks as we quietly leave the birth scene?

Jeff was born at 10:30 the night of March 7.

Every year I called Dad on March 8, the anniversary of my mother's death. Sometimes we talked about Mom, sometimes we didn't, but we knew why I called on that date. On the morning of March 8, 1985, I said, "I'm calling for the same reason I always call, and a new reason too."

"Martha, congratulations to you and Joe," he said. "Are you and the baby all right?"

"We're wonderful," I said, fighting back tears. I ached that my mother would never know this grandson, and that he would never know her. A day of death, a day of life. I was in the middle of this full cycle.

The next year, when Katie was an infant, I carried her onto our deck one warm summer night. Being under the stars makes me feel closer to my mother. I hugged my tiny daughter, her heart against mine, and I sobbed. "Mom, Katie is you. My heart is your heart. The circle is unbroken."

The rain comes down harder, and I wipe my cheeks.

Henry Higgins, it is not true that the rain in Spain falls mainly on the plain. The relatively flat regions of Castilla-León and La Rioja were hot and dry. The mountains of the northwest are the country's wettest region, and this has been our only day of rainfall. There is no shelter where we can stop to dry off, so on we go, climbing the last ascent before Santiago.

I concentrate on the muddy path, glad my tires get enough traction that I'm not slipping. We enter a eucalyptus grove. I feel like we're back in northern California on a wet November morning. Vines line the trail, and Katie picks blackberries she shares with us.

Joe has been eager to see El Rio Lavacuellos, or "Wash Your Necks River." Pilgrims wanted to clean up before they visited Santiago's shrine, and this river was the traditional place to do so. We finally reach it. The river must have been bigger a long time ago. Now it seems nothing more than a little stream mostly hidden by thick foliage. We do not claw our way through the shrubs to wash our necks. All we have to do is look down and let the rain do the washing.

We continue to climb, as do the other pilgrims on the trail with us. The camaraderie grows. We are almost there, and we are doing it in the rain. Kurt Vonnegut calls a "grand falloon" any group of people who have only one thing in common, and nothing else. His famous example: people from Indiana. I love my grand falloon of pilgrims. We are part of a thousand years' worth of humanity making this trip.

At the peak of the climb, with the rainfall letting up a bit, we take in the vista, the sprawling city of Santiago spread out in the valley before us. I don't know how many pilgrims have paused at this exact spot, but I am sure that most of them felt as I do now: it is good to be here.

Under gray skies, we descend into the city, come across a brand new Tourist Office, and reserve a hotel room for the night. We hop back on our bikes. The closer we get to the city center, the more I feel as if we've cycled into the pages of a centuries-old book. Charles Dickens' London must have looked something like this. Soot-covered stone buildings line the winding streets, jammed with pedestrians. For the first time on the Camino, the *conchas* and yellow arrows are missing, so we wander around, trying to find the cathedral that defines the end of the pilgrimage. We have crossed an entire country rarely confused about the route, and here at the destination, we can't find the ultimate landmark. Feeling like an idiot, I ask a local for directions.

At last, we spy the shrine, looking just like it does in the photos: big, brooding, and ornate. There is nothing particularly attractive or inviting about it, but no matter, this is it!

Much more vibrant is the huge plaza in front of the cathedral, teeming with camera-carrying tourists and dozens of pilgrims. Vendors hawk souvenirs. A scruffy old man who looks like a permanent pilgrim leads a heavily loaded donkey around the square. Tourists give him tips to pose with them.

Music adds to the energy. On an electric hollow-bodied guitar, a musician wearing a mask of a black man smoking a cigarette plays "Autumn Leaves," a jazz standard. Nearby, a flute player nestled in an echo-friendly stairway practices her Bach. On a road leading into the plaza, a Galician family of four is dressed in bright, traditional skirts and vests. They sing and play bagpipes, tambourine and tin whistle. Listeners and passersby make steady contributions to the tip jars.

Next to the cathedral, a lanky witch wears a gnarly mask, black dress and hat. He wields a long broom. Walking into the stream of tourists, he invites them to take a ride. One family goes for it. The witch tells them how to sit on the broomstick, and the ride begins. After a couple of bumps, the witch stands tall and the family leaps, laughing, from the stick. A few yards away, a golden angel ignores the witch. He is coated in gold from his pageboy haircut down to the small pedestal on which he perches. He stands still until a little boy comes close to get a better look. The angel blows a kiss to the boy, who giggles and runs back to parents.

A group of men rides into the square on matched gray horses. A horse trailer awaits them. I look around for, but do not see Marcel, a French masseuse we met in O Cebreiro a week ago. He'd stopped there to get shoes for his horse, who was carrying all his gear. Marcel, in contrast, was walking the Camino barefoot. Another group of men rides in, these on black horses.

In vain I look for Ana and Patricia, whom we haven't seen for days and days. I suspect our wheels have helped us get here first. They will make it, I know. *Buen Camino*, dear Spandex Ladies.

"We did it!" says Joe, giving me a hug.

"We sure did." We kiss, and Katie says, "The parents are at it again."

I turn to Katie and Jeff. "You have permanent bragging rights about this trip. You will remember this all your life, and you will tell your kids about it. Sometimes it was hot, or cold, or – "

"Stinky," Katie interrupts, and I nod.

"Sometimes it was absolutely wonderful, and sometimes absolutely grueling, but you did it. I am so proud of you! Thank you for being you!" Hugs and high fives.

I offer to take a photo of a pilgrim in front of the cathedral, and he takes one of us. I don't have to prompt anyone to smile.

"Let's go find our hotel room. We can tour the cathedral in the morning," says Joe.

As for today, we have been reminded that what matters is life – and we have it.

THE END OF THE EARTH

"This cathedral gives 'masses' a new meaning," I say to Joe as we maneuver through the throngs of tourists. They talk and laugh in this noisy, crowded mecca that feels about as holy as the Golden Arches at lunchtime on a Saturday during soccer season. Way more than the other cathedrals we've seen along the Camino, this one is crammed with gawking visitors who point at statues, paintings, hanging incense balls, and pedestals holding bowls of water. I do not recognize most of the icons and images, but it is impossible to miss the two most prominent figures.

The first is the brightly lit, golden statue of Santiago himself, dead center at the base of the altar. "Give the apostle a hug for me" is the traditional request that well-wishers ask of pilgrims. Before we get in the long line to do so, we each put our right hand in the middle of the Tree of Jesse, a column just inside the cathedral's entrance. So many pilgrims have done the same thing that five finger grooves are well worn into the marble.

Then, we begin the slow march, in single file, to enter a narrow staircase that passes behind the altar. The line climbs a few steps, and then finally, each of us passes the back of the Santiago statue.

As I watch the pilgrims in front of me reach their arms around it, I whisper to Katie, "We should wash our hands as soon as we can. Millions of people have left their germs on this statue's shoulders."

There's also a gold mollusk shell that some pilgrims kiss on the altar, but I don't mention that tradition. When my moment comes to stand behind the shining Santiago, I hug the apostle in my pajamas. This cold, drizzly day makes me glad I brought light cotton pajamas in case we slept in any of the *refugio* dorms for pilgrims. These are my only long pants, and common sense dictated I wear them today, apostle or not.

The second unmistakable figure is not Santiago the pious pilgrim, but Santiago's other self, the Moor slayer.

"That's his a-l-t-a-r ego," I say to Katie.

"Myrtle laugh."

In an imposing statue, he rides a rearing white horse that makes the Lone Ranger's Silver look like a Shetland pony. Santiago wields a sword, and three dark-skinned Muslims he's beheaded lie beneath his horse's hooves. I wonder what the nonviolent Jesus, Prince of Peace, might have felt about this warrior "saint."

I glance at windowed banks of light bulbs that look like candles. The placard invites worshippers to deposit coins, the quantity determining the wattage that will be lit.

Joe, Jeff, Katie and I leave this House of God.

We join the queue into the Pilgrim Office next door. There we can get the final stamps on our credentials, the certificates that validate our status as Pilgrims of the Camino.

While we wait, I ask, "Are you also feeling hypocritical about this?" I want the kids to beware of the danger of going through the motions when the rationale is suspect.

Joe says, "We've followed the traditions so far. We even hugged the apostle."

"One of my friends from City College came here as a tourist a few years ago. He told me he hugged the apostle, too. In his case, he's not only Jewish, but he's also…"

I pause, and Katie jumps in, "gay?"

"You guessed it. I don't think the Catholic Church would give him a hug. I don't feel right having this church give us the final stamp of approval."

"We know we made the trip for ourselves," says Joe.

We're having this conversation while we're still waiting in line.

"The other places we got our credentials stamped, I never felt like this, a supplicant among the hordes. The vibe here is different. It's as if we're giving the church the authority to confirm our success. When we look back on this moment, will we feel ridiculous, or proud, if we don't get the final stamp because of the principle of the thing? Jeff and Katie, what do you think? What would Nick and Lisa do?"

Katie says, "I think they would trust in the wisdom of their parents."

Jeff shrugs. "I don't think Nick would care that much one way or the other."

As usual, I'm the one who's making a big deal out of something. I want to defy the superstitions. I don't want our names added to a list of Catholic pilgrims maintaining reverence for the bloody Santiago. It's important that we model for the kids that principles matter. But something in me also wants to have our passports to Santiago signed, sealed, and delivered. We did it, and I want the t-shirt.

Joe says, "I think it's kind of like winning a race. You know you've won, and you don't need the medal to prove it. But still, you accept the medal."

"Thank you for finding a way to think of this so we

can have our credentials and our consciences, too."

When we get to the front of the line, we must answer a few questions. I feel as if I'm being grilled, and cringe when I say that the trip, for me, was "spiritual." I know that if I say I made it because it was the biggest family adventure we will likely ever have, I won't get the stamp. If I say this journey caused us to bond, to appreciate each other, to tolerate each other's weaknesses and help each other do more than we thought we could do, I won't get the stamp. If I say this challenge showed what we are capable of if we function as Team Kendall-Weed, I won't get the stamp. I would like to rally the dramatic gumption to refuse to add our four names to the rolls of the "spiritual" who have completed the pilgrimage to this shrine. But my idealism fails me. I say the word they need to hear, rationalizing that I'm defining "spiritual" as I choose. We walk out with our stamped credentials.

I am still spiritually clad in my pajamas, but I am far from ready for sleep.

Before we began the trip, we posted on our dining room wall the faded, well-worn map of Spain that Joe brought home with him thirty years ago. I noticed that the distance between Santiago and Finisterre, a village on the Atlantic coast, looked short. I wondered if we succeeded in getting to Santiago, maybe we might want to continue our journey and ride to Finisterre – which means "The End of the Earth" – the westernmost point on the Iberian Peninsula.

To explore this possibility, we walk to Santiago's downtown tourist office, barely a block away. I feel smug telling the clerk my idea to continue going west, and I ask for maps she might have to guide us to the coast.

"Certainly." she replies. "The trail is well marked."

"The trail?"

"Yes, the Camino continues to Finisterre. The *conchas* and arrows point the way."

"So much for my original idea," I mumble to Joe.

"Our adventure can continue," says Joe, smiling at Jeff and Katie. "What do you think?"

"Let's go ridin'," says Jeff.

"Let's just not get up too early tomorrow morning," says Katie.

At the tourist office we get the name of the only hotel in Negreira, the largest town in the one hundred kilometers between Santiago and Finisterre. We make reservations at the hotel for the next night. As for this evening, we walk the narrow streets to choose a restaurant for dinner.

Sandwich boards on the sidewalks, one after another, advertise *pulpo*, which means "octopus." In window displays, dead specimens sprawl grotesquely, their long tentacles intertwined with glassy-eyed fish and plastic flowers. Because so many restaurants are bragging about their *pulpo*, I suspect this is either a regional or seasonal specialty.

"Let's try it," says Jeff. I smile weakly in support of his open-mindedness. We pick a restaurant and go in.

It seems to me that octopus is likely to resemble calamari, which Joe loves, but I have judged to be squiggly, rubbery, and yucky. Joe and Jeff order the *pulpo* special.

As I'm struggling to overcome my provincialism and be a role model who tries new things, Katie says, "I don't think I even need to consider eating that." Thank you, honey. She and I chicken out, literally. We all trade bites. Nobody is wild about the food, no matter which plate the bites are taken from. But we eat heartily, a fueling necessity.

At bedtime back at our hotel, I finally take off my pajamas.

I don't need them the next day, as the warm sunshine invites Joe and me to don shorts and sunscreen. The kids are sleeping in. Joe and I rent a van, and we drive it to Finisterre, where we will park it for the night. We'll need the van to drive from Finisterre to Madrid for our flight home.

We return to Santiago on a bus, and it is not until late afternoon that the four of us get back on the cycling trail. As we pedal past the Cathedral one last time and pick up the Camino to head for Negreira, 22 kilometers away, I tell the Team, "I've been waiting weeks to say this. Finally I can. I will ride to the end of the earth with you."

Leaving Santiago, we discover that although the tourist office is right that the trail continues, almost nobody uses it. At first, it wends through a eucalyptus forest, but soon deposits us on single track that is overgrown with stickery brambles that prick my arms and legs. We see no other pilgrims. The trail is rugged and uneven, with lots of hummocky ups and downs. Several times we have to get off our bikes to shove them across rocky streams or up slippery hills. At the top of one of them, we pause while Katie adjusts a pannier that has come loose.

I say, "I love you through thicket and thin." When at first no one responds, Joe doesn't leave me in the lurch.

"Myrtle laugh," he says.

The dusk deepens. We have avoided riding after dark for the entire trip, but we weren't able to start today until almost six p.m. The earth hasn't slowed its rotation to accommodate our logistics. We pedal across a narrow stone bridge that I hope marks the entrance to Negreira.

No such luck. In front of a renovated two-story stone building, a BMW is parked on the narrow road. The only car in sight, it seems totally out of place. Horses and farm wagons seem more in keeping with the feel of this ancient cluster of stone buildings with sagging roofs. Tall, old, mossy trees bend toward the stream we just crossed. I wonder if this fixed-up house might be part of the beginning of suburban development near Santiago. A woman sticks her head out the upstairs window and waves to us. "Good evening," we say. I'd love to quiz her about this town, her life, and this car, but of course, we just keep riding.

We pedal past a field of black and white cows. They all face the same direction, like boats tied to buoys on a windy afternoon.

Finally we cycle into Negreira, a town larger than I expected. Its streetlights turn on just as we arrive, a most welcomed welcome.

The dining room at our two-star Hotel Tamara is quite full. It appears that several large groups are eating here, with many tables shoved together. The chairs are all encased in off-white slipcovers that hide their legs. They look like the little sorcerers in Disney's film *The Sorcerer's Apprentice*. Only one meal choice is offered, and it's delicious – salad, roasted meat (as usual for the menu of the day, I can't tell what the meat is, but I don't think it is *pulpo)*, vegetables, rice, bread, ice cream for dessert, and beverages (water, lemon soda, a bottle of red wine and a bottle of white wine). The total bill for all four of us? Twenty-four euros! That's less than thirty dollars. Nowhere have we found food or wine to be expensive, but this is the cheapest we've seen. We may be on an extension of the Camino, but we are clearly off the beaten track.

The next morning, as I'm putting my panniers on my bike, now a routine procedure, my eye catches motion in the shrubs beside the hotel's parking lot.

"There's a robin!" I call out. The European version is smaller and has less rufous on its breast than the American kind. I don't hear it sing "cheerio," so I do.

"Cheerio, cheerio, let's go!" Jeff and Katie pretend they hear nothing, know no one, and only coincidentally happen to be standing near me.

Cool damp air and anticipation energize what I expect will be our last day on the Camino. After almost three weeks of all-day, every day exercise, I am in the best physical shape I've ever been in. As for emotional shape, my mood is as up and down as the terrain.

Writer May Sarton says that being in the presence of another person always alters an experience. Partly for that reason, she prefers the solitary life. Unlike her, I generally prefer the shared experience. I would never have made this trip alone. Joking with Katie, seeing Jeff shine in his role as bike mechanic, watching Joe delight in our immersion in the culture – their pleasure enhances mine. Our synergy reminds me of the high I enjoyed one evening in our living room when Joe and I played with Tom Rigney, a Berkeley fiddler. Joe is a world-class player of melodies, and Tom is a world-class player of rhythms. Standing between these two masters, I lost my sense of self, with my fingers and soul so liberated that I fiddled better than I know how.

But life is change, and endings help us cherish the present. This pilgrimage will end when the earth does, in Finisterre. Although Joe and I drove the rented van there yesterday, we haven't really *been* there. We have saved our "first time" for our family's arrival on our bicycles.

When the four of us pedal to the top of the last

mountain ridge on the way to the coast, we stop to take in the panorama of the curving shoreline and the sparkling ocean beneath a perfect deep blue sky.

Jeff says, "This looks just like home!"

"No matter where we go, there we are," I answer.

We cruise the descent and then cycle north along the coast toward the town of Finisterre. It seems odd to pass families vacationing at the shore. For us, this is the culmination of an odyssey. For them, it is a day at the beach.

"Let's stop," I broadcast into my radio.

"Why?" asks Jeff.

"We need to dip our toes into the Atlantic. When you come to another beach, please wait for us."

"We've already been in the Atlantic, at Grandpa Florida's," says Katie as she pulls up next to me.

"I know, but that was the American side. This is the other side. It's a symbolic thing."

Jeff stops where there is beach access, and we join him.

"Lewis and Clark dipped their feet into the Pacific," says Joe.

"Sacajawea did too," I say. Then I grin at Katie. "Pocahontas, want to join me?"

We shove our bikes across the sand. Since this was my big idea, I put my hand in first. The water is freezing. The kids indulge me, each briefly touching the water, and then shaking their cold, wet hands off on each other.

We continue riding north toward the main street of Finisterre, a picturesque fishing village all year long and a modest resort during the summer months. We are here! I'm pedaling on the level, but my chest heaves. Yes, we have done it! My family, I, we, have done it! How can life be this good?

I slow down and wait for Joe, who's as usual cycling in the rear. I do my best to grin at him, but I suspect my face shows my emotional overload. He smiles quickly but immediately raises the video camera to save the moment, and perhaps to save face, too.

Quit thinking. Just ride!

This destination is no tourist-jammed shrine to a Moorkiller. Finisterre is filled with affirmations of life. Swooping flocks of gulls squawk like they own the place, as they do. Cool moist salty air makes the hot dry plains almost impossible to remember. The little harbor is crowded with bobbing red, yellow, green and blue fishing boats and rowboats moored close together.

Skinny young boys in skimpy swimsuits are jumping off the public pier. For them, this must be a warm day. I ask one of the kids to snap our picture. He does not need to say "Smile!" None of us could do anything else.

I thank him, and we hop back on our bikes. The village road ends just past the harbor. We lay our bikes down and clamber to the top of boulders along the cliff. At this lookout point, we savor the sunny, breezy vista of the Atlantic Ocean, our last stop of this journey.

I scramble back to my bike. From my pannier I pull out a wrinkled little plastic bag that has bounced for almost a thousand kilometers from Roncesvalles to this moment. It contains four small stones that I gathered a lifetime ago at a Pacific beach not far from home so that we could toss them, if we made it all the way, into the Atlantic at the End of the Earth.

I hold out the bag to Joe, Jeff and Katie. "Pick your pebble." My voice quivers. "We have made this trip what it is, and we make this family what we are. Who wants to go first?"

Katie says, "Mom and Dad, you go."

Joe and I hold hands and carefully toss our stones in unison. Then Jeff and Katie step to the edge of the cliff and toss their stones with joyous abandon. Confident youth, you have it all.

I have it all, too.

Thirty-two years ago, Joe vowed, "One day, I will do it." Do I feel glad that he keeps his promises? I sure do.

Buen Camino.

AFTERWARD

Even though eight years have passed since we cycled the Camino, I can still hear the contents of my handle bar bag bouncing and jumbling as I pedaled rough trails, feel the grit clinging to my ankles as we sweated across the arid plains, and taste the crisp white wine that I savored at the end of each exhausting and exhilarating day.

Since then, Katie has graduated from Cal State Long Beach with a double major in English Literature and Creative Writing, and a minor in Women's Studies. She just earned a Master's in Screenwriting at Cal State Northridge, and is pursuing her dream of becoming a rock star. She is the fiddler in Old Man Markley, a punk bluegrass band in Los Angeles.

Jeff graduated from Cal Poly, San Luis Obispo, with a major in English, a certificate in TESOL, and a minor in Spanish. He spent his junior year at the University of Alicante in southern Spain. When he was seventeen, his goals were to have a truck and a girlfriend, and to work in the bike industry. In his Ford Ranger, now he and his girlfriend drive to Downhill Mountain Bike races where Jeff competes as a pro. He works at Ibis Cycles in Santa Cruz.

Joe continues to produce CDs, soundtracks and DVDs. Most recently, he made a documentary film *The Waltz to Westphalia.* It's the biography of a classic fiddle waltz. He also produced a CD of music referenced in Laura Ingalls Wilder's *Little House* series. It's called *Pa's Fiddle.*

On the Camino, Joe and I discovered how much we like to spin our wheels. In 2005 he and I rode across Missouri on the 225-mile Katy Trail. In 2006 we visited Jeff in

Alicante. After putting him on a bus to Germany to compete in a World Cup bike race, Joe and I cycled 650 miles on the Via de la Plata from Sevilla in southern Spain to Santiago. In 2008 we rode from Washington, D.C. to Pittsburgh, PA, on the historic C & O Canal Towpath and the GAP trail. Most recently, we cycled the Camino del Norte, a 550-mile route from Irún at the French border across the northern Spanish coast to Santiago.

How much have I missed the kids? To cope with our empty nest, I busied myself by writing three teacher resource books about conflict resolution, a biography of Herbert Hoover for Scholastic, an updated biography of Jane Goodall, and two books for National Geographic: *The Erie Canal* and *Alive in the Killing Fields, Surviving the Khmer Rouge Genocide*. At San Jose City College, I became the Coordinator of the Teaching and Learning Center, Coordinator of Learning Communities, Chair of the English Department, and finally Dean of Language Arts. Upon my retirement in August, 2009 at age 62, Joe urged me to revisit my Camino manuscript, which I had set aside. With many thanks for his encouragement, I am delighted to see this memoir come to fruition. Joe continues to be my Mr. Right.

Reading Group Questions
and
Topics for Discussion

1. What challenges does this family face in their ride across Spain?

2. To what extent does Team Kendall-Weed seem like a typical American family?

3. What is the biggest adventure your family has embarked on? What were its challenges and rewards?

4. How might this memoir differ if it were told from the perspective of Joe, Jeff or Katie?

5. Marty, the narrator, considers herself a feminist. How do you define “feminist”?

6. What qualities make a good teacher? In what ways do the skills needed for good teaching and parenting overlap?

7. Marty mentions several uses of language that have particular meaning within her family, such as “wow,” “yikes,” and “Myrtle laugh.” What words or sayings have special significance in your family?

8. Do you speak a language in addition to English? If so, can you think of examples of words or expressions in that language that can't be translated easily into English, or vice versa?

9. Marty claims that rules and boundaries can provide opportunities for creative expression in art, music or poetry. Do you agree? If so, what examples come to mind?

10. Take a close look at the sonnet Marty writes at Katie's urging. Note how it follows the structure: 14 lines, each in iambic pentameter. Read it aloud, exaggerating the rhymes at the end of each line, as well as the "da-DUM" rhythm. Then read it more naturally, with the rhythm a subtle undercurrent to the text, almost like the regular rotation of bike wheels. You might want to try your hand at composing a sonnet, too.

11. Marty criticizes herself for her inadequate cycling skills. Do you feel sympathetic to her worries, impatient with her lack of confidence, or … ? Can you think of activities you've tried but felt nervous about? If you succeeded, how did you overcome your anxiety?

12. When shopping for clothes in the mountain town of Sarria, Marty feels shy in the foreign environment. Have you experienced culture shock, and what was it like?

13. Human beings seem to crave risk, but something that is satisfying for one person may be terrifying for another, such as speaking in front of a group, exhibiting a work of art, skiing down a steep slope, or committing to a

relationship. Consider the risks mentioned in this book, and compare them with risks you have taken. What do you suppose is the appeal of risk taking?

14. Marty dreads Jeff and Katie's loss of childhood, and the resulting changes in her role as mother. Do you think she seems normal in this feeling, or is she clinging to a past she needs to let go?

15. Marty often reflects on her role as a college teacher of literature. Is she fortunate to care so much about her profession, or does she seem like a workaholic? What are advantages and disadvantages of having a job that stays at the office as opposed to having a job that is central to someone's identity?

16. What themes appear in the book? Do they seem universal, applying to people everywhere?

17. Marty sometimes feels impatient while Joe compares many hotel options before they choose one. She refers to him as a perfectionist. In your experience, have you noticed differences in people's decision-making processes? Is friction the inevitable result, or can such differences help to balance a relationship?

18. What does it mean to be a "saint"? Marty is critical of the warrior side of Santiago. Can you think of other examples of religious role models who were violent? Is there a contradiction between wielding a sword and attaining sainthood as you define it?

19. Marty is reluctant to call her journey "spiritual," a

requirement for getting the final stamp on her Camino credential at the pilgrims' office in Santiago. How does she justify her decision? Explain why you would or would not have made the same one. What is the difference between spirituality and religiosity?

20. Based on this memoir, what are your impressions of Spain? If you have visited that country, compare your experiences with those described here.

Would you like to invite the author to speak to your group? Contact her at www.MarthaKendall.com.

For information about Joe's music, see www.JoeWeed.com.

LaVergne, TN USA
25 March 2011
221467LV00003B/211/P

9 780945 783190